Berklee Practice Method

GUITAR

Get Your Band Together

LARRY BAIONE

and the

Berklee Faculty

Berklee Press

Director: Dave Kusek
Managing Editor: Debbie Cavalier
Marketing Manager: Ola Frank
Sr. Writer/Editor: Jonathan Feist
Writer/Editor: Susan Gedutis
Product Manager: Ilene Altman

ISBN 0-634-00649-5

1140 Boylston Street
Boston, MA 02215-3693 USA
(617) 747-2146

Visit Berklee Press Online at
www.berkleepress.com

DISTRIBUTED BY

HAL•LEONARD®
CORPORATION
7777 W. BLUEMOUND RD. P.O. BOX 13819
MILWAUKEE, WISCONSIN 53213

Visit Hal Leonard Online at
www.halleonard.com

DESIGN TEAM

Matt Marvuglio	Curriculum Editor Dean of the Professional Performance Division
Jonathan Feist	Series Editor Senior Writer/Editor, Berklee Press
Rich Appleman	Chair of the Bass Department
Larry Baione	Chair of the Guitar Department
Jeff Galindo	Assistant Professor of Brass
Matt Glaser	Chair of the String Department
Russell Hoffmann	Assistant Professor of Piano
Charles Lewis	Associate Professor of Brass
Jim Odgren	Academic Advising Coordinator
Tiger Okoshi	Associate Professor of Brass
Bill Pierce	Chair of the Woodwind Department
Tom Plsek	Chair of the Brass Department
Mimi Rabson	Assistant Professor of Strings
John Repucci	Assistant Chair of the Bass Department
Ed Saindon	Assistant Professor of Percussion
Ron Savage	Chair of the Ensemble Department
Casey Scheuerell	Associate Professor of Percussion
Paul Schmeling	Chair of the Piano Department
Jan Shapiro	Chair of the Voice Department

The Band

Rich Appleman, Bass
Larry Baione, Guitar
Jim Odgren, Alto Sax
Casey Scheuerell, Drums
Paul Schmeling, Keyboard

Music composed by Matt Marvuglio.

Recording produced and engineered by Rob Jaczko,
Chair of the Music Production and Engineering Department.

Contents

CD Tracks

Basics

CD 1. "Tuning Notes"

Chapter I. Playing Rock ("Sweet")

CD 2. "Sweet" Full Band
CD 3. "Sweet" First Part
CD 4. "Sweet" Second Part
CD 5. "Sweet" Guitar/Bass
CD 6. "Sweet" Call/Response 1
CD 7. "Sweet" Call/Response 2
CD 8. "Sweet" You're the Guitar

Chapter II. Playing Blues ("Do It Now")

CD 9. "Do It Now" Full Band
CD 10. "Do It Now" Guitar Comping
CD 11. "Do It Now" No Melody
CD 12. "Do It Now" Call/Response 1
CD 13. "Do It Now" Call/Response 2
CD 14. "Do It Now" You're the Guitar

Chapter III. Playing Swing ("I Just Wanna Be With You")

CD 15. "I Just Wanna Be With You" Full Band
CD 16. "I Just Wanna Be With You" You're the Guitar
CD 17. "I Just Wanna Be With You" Call/Response 1
CD 18. "I Just Wanna Be With You" Call/Response 2
CD 19. "I Just Wanna Be With You" Call/Response: Licks

Chapter IV. Playing Funk ("Leave Me Alone")

CD 20. "Leave Me Alone" Full Band
CD 21. "Leave Me Alone" You're the Guitar
CD 22. "Leave Me Alone" Call/Response 1
CD 23. "Leave Me Alone" Call/Response 2

Foreword

Berklee College of Music has been training musicians for over fifty years. Our graduates go onto successful careers in the music business, and many have found their way to the very top of the industry, producing hit records, receiving the highest awards, and sharing their music with millions of people.

An important reason why Berklee is so successful is that our curriculum stresses the practical application of musical principles. Our students spend a lot of time playing together in bands. When you play with other musicians, you learn things that are impossible to learn in any other way. Teachers are invaluable, practicing by yourself is critical, but performing in a band is the most valuable experience of all. That's what is so special about this series: it gives you the theory you need, but also prepares you to play in a band.

The goal of the *Berklee Practice Method* is to present some of Berklee's teaching strategies in book and audio form. The chairs of each of our instrumental departments—guitar, bass, keyboard, percussion, woodwind, brass, string, and voice—have gotten together and discussed the best ways to teach you how to play in a band. They teamed with some of our best faculty and produced a set of books with play-along audio tracks that uniquely prepares its readers to play with other musicians.

Students who want to study at Berklee come from a variety of backgrounds. Some have great technique, but have never improvised. Some have incredible ears, but need more work on their reading skills. Some have a very creative, intuitive sense of music, but their technical skills aren't strong enough, yet, to articulate their ideas.

The *Berklee Practice Method* teaches many of these different aspects of musicianship. It is the material that our faculty wishes all Berklee freshmen could master before arriving on our doorstep.

When you work through this book, don't just read it. You've got to play through every example, along with the recording. Better yet, play them with your own band.

Playing music with other people is how you will learn the most. This series will help you master the skills you need to become a creative, expressive, and supportive musician that anyone would want to have in their band.

Gary Burton
Executive Vice President,
Berklee College of Music

Preface

Thank you for choosing the *Berklee Practice Method* for guitar. This book/CD package, developed by the faculty of Berklee College of Music, is part of the *Berklee Practice Method* series—the instrumental method that teaches how to play in a band.

The recording included with this method provides an instant band you can play along with, featuring great players from Berklee's performance faculty. Each tune has exercises and practice tracks that will help prepare you to play it. Rock, blues, and funk are just some of the styles you will perform.

The lessons in this book will guide you through chord voicings, chord changes, scales, improvisation techniques, rhythm accompaniments, tablature, and traditional notation. As you progress through each chapter, traditional notation becomes the focus (this will prepare you better for real-life gigging situations). It is intended for guitarists who are just beginning lessons with their teacher, though guitarists learning on their own will also find it invaluable.

You should have some knowledge of the fretboard and the basics of playing guitar. These are reviewed in the "Basics" chapter.

Most importantly, you will learn the skills you need to play guitar in a band. Play along with the recording, and play with your friends. This series coordinates methods for many different instruments, and all are based on the same tunes, in the same keys. If you know a drummer, horn player, etc., have them pick up the *Berklee Practice Method* for their own instruments, and then you can jam together.

Work hard, make music, have fun!

Larry Baione
Chair of the Guitar Department
Berklee College of Music

Basics

Before you start chapter 1, you should understand the following topics.

PARTS OF A GUITAR

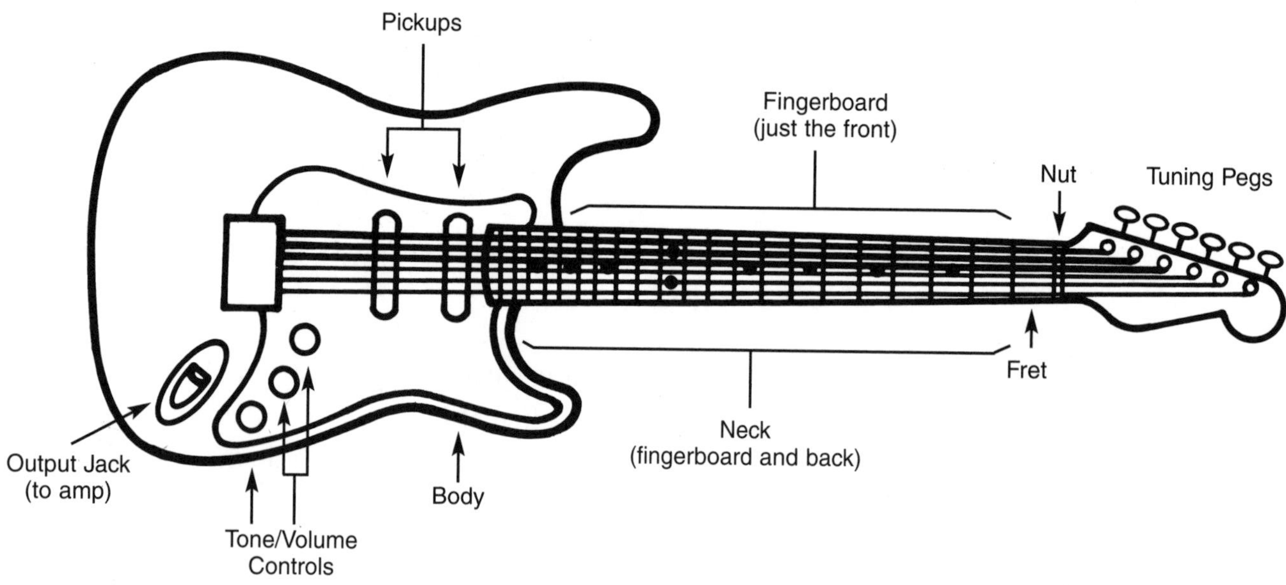

PLUGGING IN

To protect your equipment and your ear drums, follow these steps when you plug into an amp.

1. Turn off the amp, and set the volume on the amp and the guitar down to 0.
2. Plug your 1/4" cable into your guitar and then into the amp.
3. Turn on the amp.
4. Turn up the guitar volume all the way.
5. Slowly, turn up the amp volume until it is loud enough.

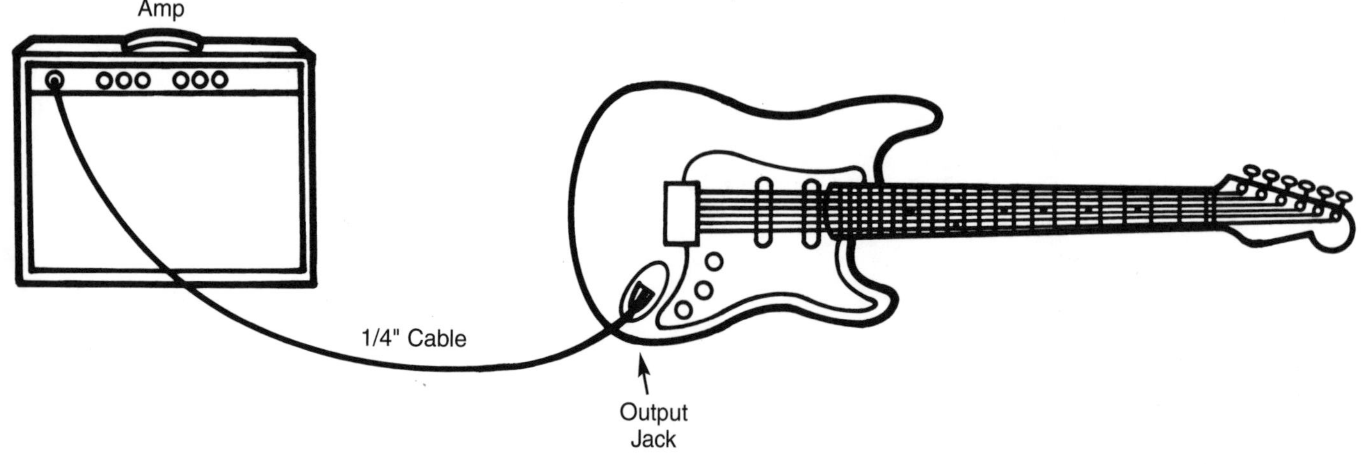

HOLDING THE GUITAR

Whether you are standing or sitting, your guitar should be in the same position in relation to your body. This lets you keep the same hand position all the time, and helps you play more consistently. Point the guitar neck upward at a 45-degree angle. Its back should lean against the lower part of your chest. Its height and angle should always be the same, whether you are sitting or standing. Your hands shouldn't support any weight. They have enough to do playing the notes. When you're sitting, rest the guitar on whichever leg feels most comfortable for you. A strap helps keep your guitar in position. A foot rest makes it more comfortable to play while seated.

PRACTICE TIP

Good playing technique means more stamina, more facility, and a better sound. You will avoid injuries, which can be painful and even force you to stop playing. Ask an experienced guitarist to review your playing position and make sure that you are on the right track. Remember, if it hurts, you should correct it right away.

HANDS

Left Hand

Your left-hand fingers hold down the strings to sound the correct pitches. Your hand should be comfortable and never feel strained.

Finger Numbers

Finger numbers go from one to four, from the index finger to the pinkie. Your thumb is just "your thumb."

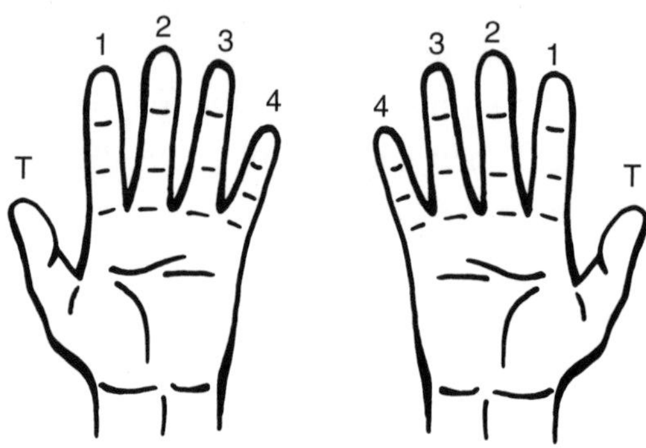

Right Hand: Using a Pick

Most rock and jazz guitarists use a pick. Picks help you play fast, crisp notes, which are generally preferred for these styles.

Hold the pick between your thumb and the first knuckle of your index finger. A long side of the pick should be parallel with the side of your thumb. Using the long side helps get the most contact with the string. Hold the pick with enough pressure that you don't drop it, but not so tightly that you feel any tension in your hand. Again, you should feel comfortable.

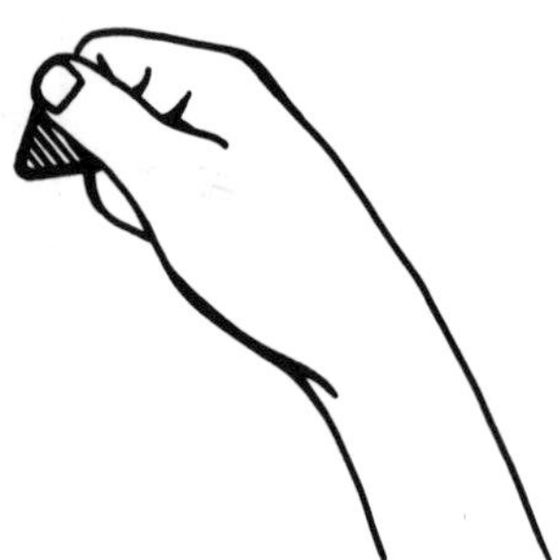

Rest your right forearm comfortably on the top or side of the guitar so that your right hand is between the pickups if your guitar is electric, or over the sound hole if it is acoustic.

Using a Pick

To play ("pick") a note, move the pick downwards—not outward—to pluck the string. Come to a rest on the next string (or about that distance, if you are playing on the first string). This is called a *downstroke*, sometimes notated with the symbol: ⊓.

An *upstroke* is the opposite—pluck the string upwards with a flick of the wrist (be sure not to move your whole arm). It is notated with the symbol: V. Sometimes you will want to alternate upstrokes and downstrokes. This is called *alternate picking*.

STRINGS

The guitar has six strings—from lowest to highest sounding: E, A, D, G, B, E.

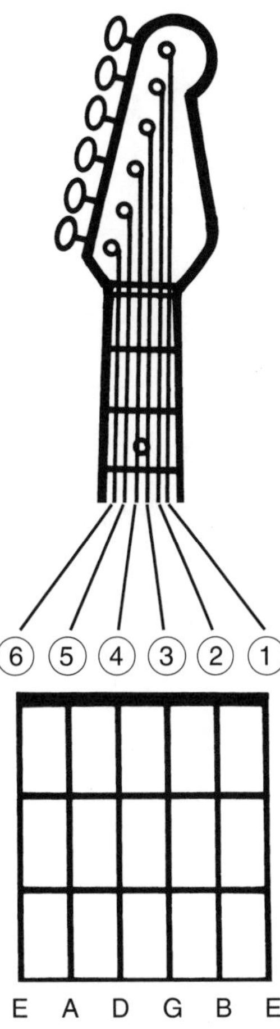

TUNING

Before you play, tune your strings to the right notes. If your string is flat (too loose), tighten its tuning peg to raise the pitch. If your string is sharp (too tight), loosen its tuning peg to lower the pitch. As you get close to the right pitch, listen for *beats* (tiny waves of sound) as you play your note along with the correctly tuned note. Slight differences in pitch causes these audible beats. Keep tuning until you don't hear any beats.

There are many ways to tune. One of the most convenient is using an electric tuner. You can also tune by ear, using this recording.

Tuning to the *Berklee Practice Method* Recording

1. Listen to "Tuning Note E."

2. Play your high E string. Determine whether the pitch of your E string is above or below the pitch on the recording. Don't worry if you can't tell, at first. Just try moving the tuning peg slowly, in either direction, until is sounds right.

3. While your string is still sounding its note, turn the E string's tuning peg until it is at the same pitch as the recorded tuning note. Pluck it again every few seconds, and keep listening closely until it is tuned.

4. When the high E string is tuned, tune the B, G, D, A, and low E strings to the pitches on the tuning track.

Your guitar should now be in tune.

NOTATION

Guitar players read three kinds of notation: tablature, chord frames, and traditional notation.

Tablature

Tablature (or "tab") has six lines, one for each string. Fret numbers show which fret you should hold down.

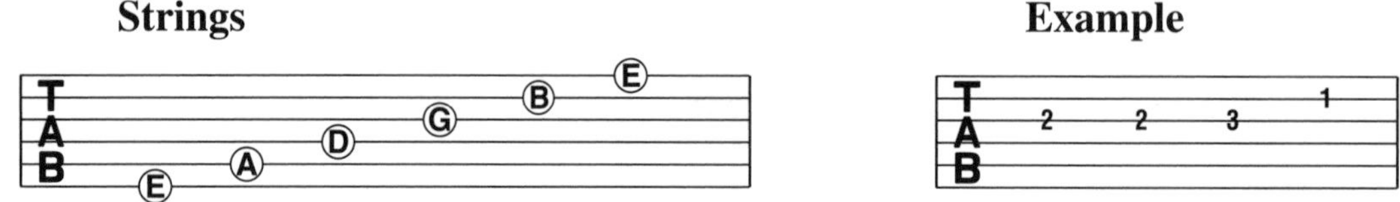

Chord Frames

Chord frames show fingerings for chords. Hold down the strings where you see the dots.

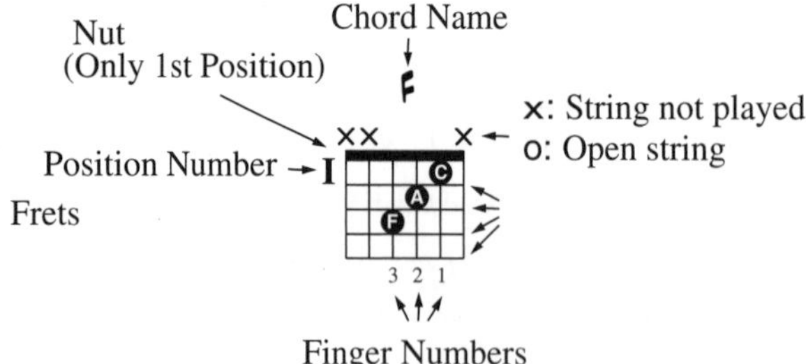

Traditional Notation

Notes are written on a staff.

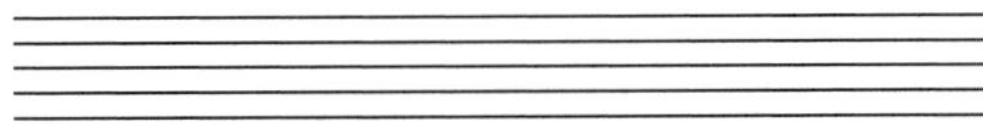

Guitar music is usually written using the "treble clef" staff. Here are the notes for the lines and spaces in treble clef.

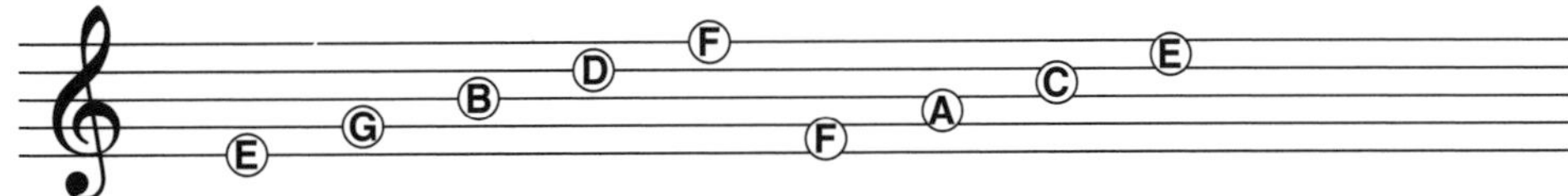

Ledger Lines

The staff can be extended with ledger lines.

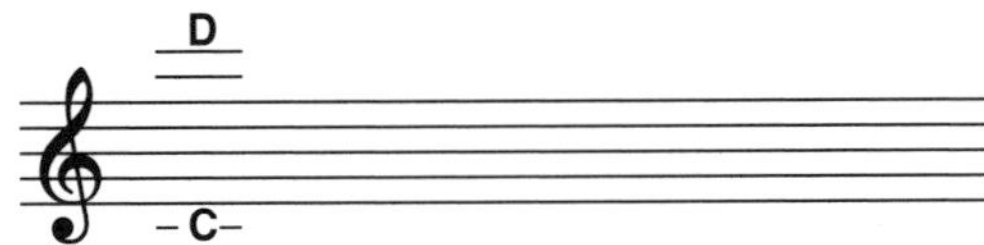

String Numbers

Circled numbers above the staff indicate the string to use for that note (and the notes that follow it). Strings are numbered from highest to lowest: low E is considered the sixth string, high E is called the first string. These numbers are similar to tab, in that they indicate what string to use for a note. In this example, the tab and the circles indicate the same thing. Generally, you will see either one or the other, but you should be able to read both types of notation.

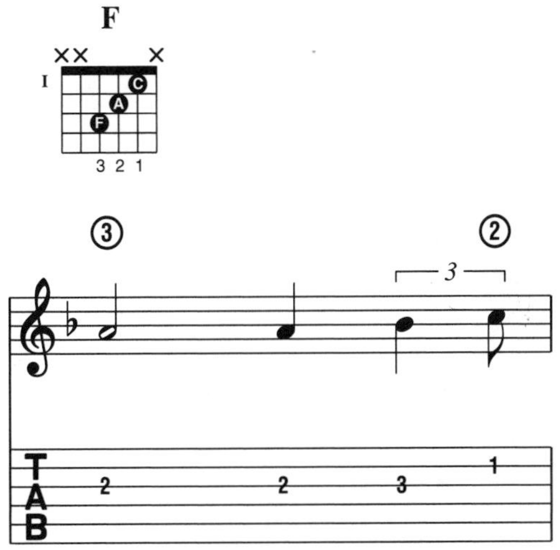

PRACTICE TIPS

- Tab often appears beneath regular notation. You can use tab to learn how to finger the note.
- Traditional notation shows rhythms, note names, and musical nuances.
- Chord frames may appear above the staff. Use chord frames to learn chord fingerings.

ACCIDENTALS

Accidentals are symbols appearing before notes, showing that a pitch is raised or lowered for the duration of the measure, unless otherwise indicated.

♭	Flat	Next note down (half step, or one fret down)
♯	Sharp	Next note up (half step, or one fret up)
♮	Natural	Cancels a flat or sharp

KEY SIGNATURES

Key signatures indicate a tune's key and show which notes always get sharps or flats. Accidentals on the lines and spaces in the key signature affect those notes throughout the tune unless there is a natural sign. Here are some key signatures used in this book.

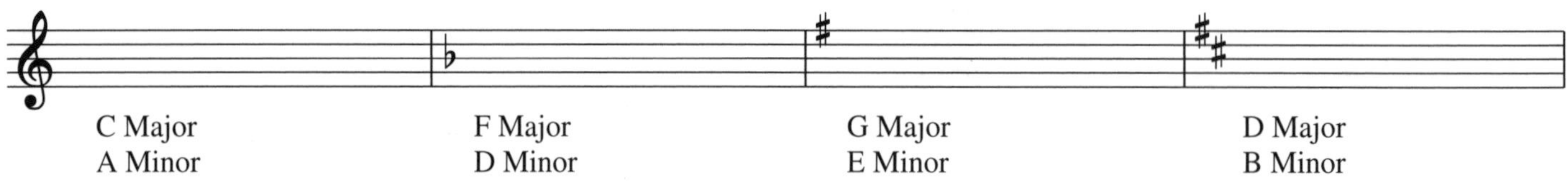

C Major
A Minor

F Major
D Minor

G Major
E Minor

D Major
B Minor

RHYTHMS

Below are the basic rhythms. When there are no actual pitches, as in a clapping exercise, rhythms may be shown on the *percussion clef.* (The beats are numbered below the staff).

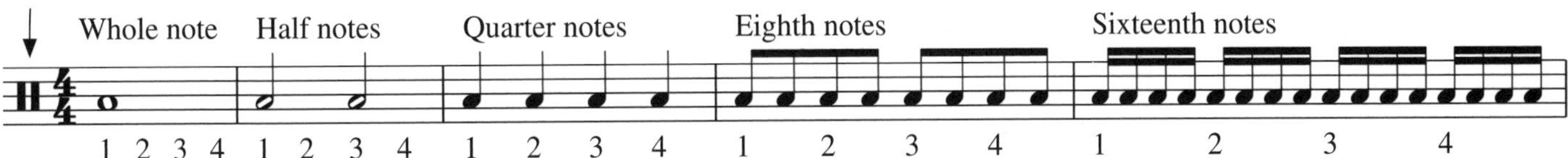

Connect notes using a tie. The first note is held for a total of six beats.

Extend a note's rhythmic value by using a dot. A dot increases the value by one half.

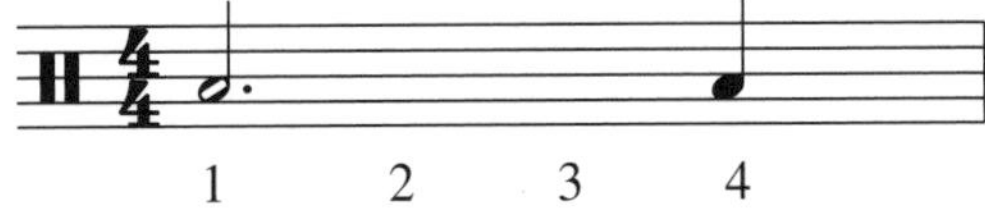

Triplets squeeze three even notes into the space of two. In this example, the quarter-note beat is divided first into two eighth notes, and then into three eighth-note triplets.

RHYTHMIC NOTATION

Music that just shows rhythms may be written in rhythmic notation. This is common in rhythm exercises, where the emphasis is on rhythm, not on which notes you should play. The stems are the same, but the noteheads are different.

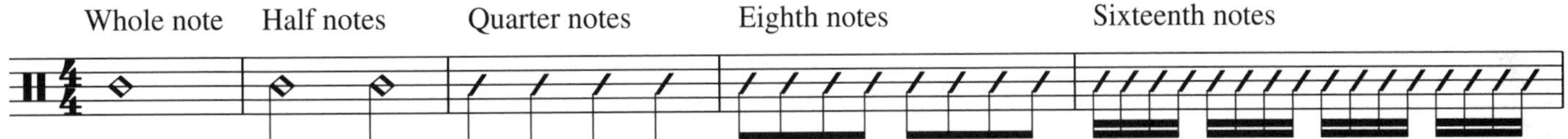

x noteheads are used for percussive sounds, such as a clapping, or strumming dampened strings.

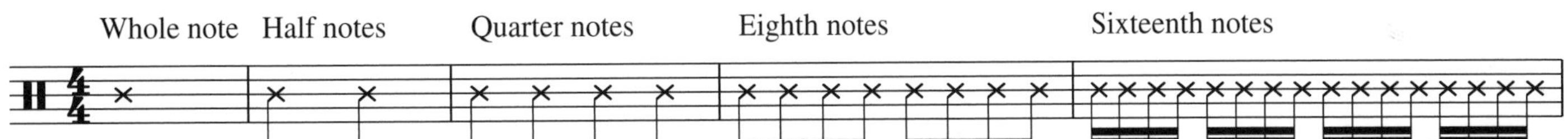

MEASURES

Groups of beats are divided into measures. Measure lengths are shown with *time signatures.* This measure is in $\frac{4}{4}$ time—there are four quarter notes in the measure, and the quarter note gets the beat.

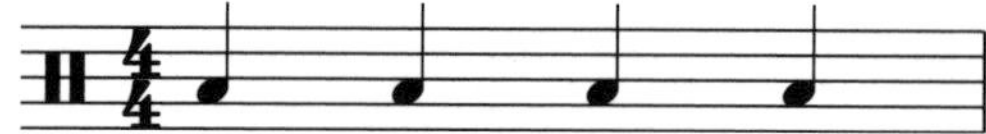

In $\frac{12}{8}$ time, there are twelve eighth notes per measure and the eighth note gets the beat. (Often, $\frac{12}{8}$ is felt as four beats, with three lesser beats inside each.)

ARTICULATIONS

Articulations give more information about how to play a note. Here are four common ones used in this book:

>	Accent	Loud
.	Staccato	Short
^	Short	Short and loud
–	Long	Hold for full value

Now, let's play!

PLAYING ROCK

CHAPTER I

"Sweet" is a *rock* tune. Rock started in the 1960s and has roots in blues, swing, r&b, and rock 'n' roll. There are many different styles of rock. To hear more rock, listen to artists such as Rage Against the Machine, Melissa Etheridge, Korn, Paula Cole, Bjork, Tori Amos, Primus, Jimi Hendrix, and Led Zeppelin.

LESSON 1
TECHNIQUE/THEORY

Listen to "Sweet" on the recording. This tune has two main parts. The guitar parts are shown below with notes only, no rhythms.

In the first part, the guitar plays this:

In the second part, the guitar plays this:

Play along with the recording and try to match the guitar. Notice that there is a short introduction before the first part begins.

POWER CHORDS

In the first part of "Sweet," the guitar plays *power chords*, doubling the bass. A power chord is two notes played at the same time, a fifth (five notes) apart. They are usually played in the lower range of the guitar on the fifth and sixth strings.

Power chords have an open sound that is typical of rock music. They are simple and strong, and sound good cranked at any volume.

Chord symbols for power chords are the bottom note with a "5," showing that the high note is a fifth above the root. So, the chord symbol for a power chord with the root E is "E5." Here are the three power chords used for the first part, with their symbols:

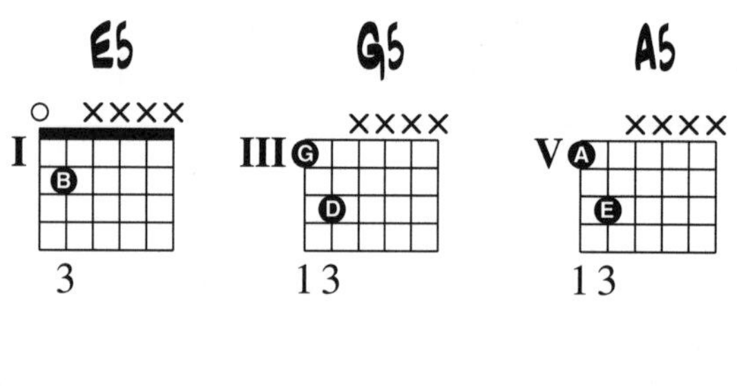

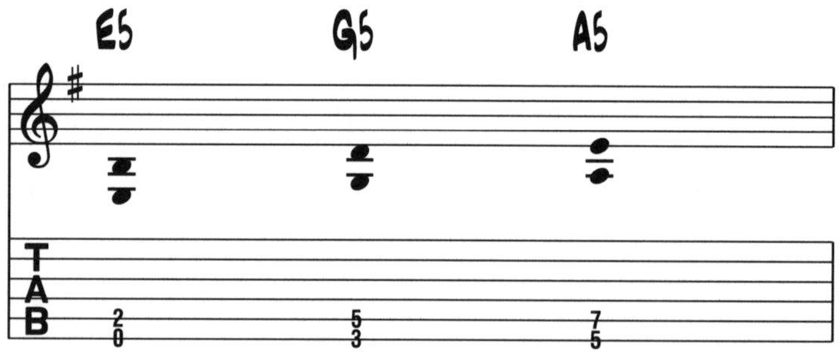

Listen to the first part to "Sweet." Imitate the guitar part, taking turns playing licks with the recording. Try to match its rhythm. Practice these power chords until you can play them easily.

SECOND LICK

Listen to the second part to "Sweet." Finger the A on the E string, using the fingering shown. Use alternate picking, switching upstrokes and downstrokes on every note, and starting each five-note grouping with a downstroke. Again, practice this alone, until you can play it comfortably, and then play along with the recording.

LEAD SHEETS

When you play in a band, your sheet music might show just chord symbols and melody. This is called a *lead sheet.* Lead sheets tell which chords to play along with the melody. The whole band may read the same lead sheet. Each player will use it differently to create a part for their individual instrument. This is what the first part of "Sweet" looks like on a lead sheet.

Notice that there is no G chord on the lead sheet. The G power chord linking the E– and A chords was added by the guitarist on the recording. If he wanted to, he could just play the E and A power chords, but this way is more interesting.

PERFORMANCE TIP

Chord symbols don't specify any rhythms. They don't even tell you exactly what notes to play. They just tell you, "Play an E minor chord." You can play it in any way that you want, as long as it fits in, or *hooks up*, with what the rest of the band is playing.

Different guitar players will create different parts to the same tune. This is one of the coolest things about lead-sheet notation: it leaves room for individual interpretation.

This is what the lead sheet looks like for the second part:

You will see the full lead sheet to "Sweet" in lesson 4.

LESSON 2
LEARNING THE GROOVE

WHAT IS A GROOVE?

A *groove* is a combination of musical patterns in which everyone in the band feels and plays to a common pulse. This creates a sense of unity and momentum. The *rhythm section* (usually drums, bass, guitar, and keyboard) lays down the groove's dynamic and rhythmic feel. A singer or soloist also contributes to the groove and performs the melody based on this feel.

LISTEN 2 PLAY

Listen to "Sweet." As is common in hard rock, the groove to "Sweet" has a strong, clear pulse, and a loud, forceful sound. The drums play a heavy, repetitive beat. The bass outlines the harmonic structure. The guitar and keyboards play chords. Everyone uses the same rhythms, though often at different times. This makes the whole band sound like one unit; they're all *hooked up* with the groove.

In lesson 1, when you played along with the recording and matched the guitar part, you hooked into a groove and became part of the rhythm section.

LEAD GUITAR AND RHYTHM GUITAR

Guitarists have two roles in a band: lead guitar and rhythm guitar. The *lead guitar* part plays melodies and improvises solos. The *rhythm guitar* part plays chords or riffs that back up someone else who plays melody or sings. Sometimes, a band will have different guitarists playing each part, and sometimes, a single guitarist will alternate between them. All guitarists should be able to play both. On this recording, "Sweet" has just a rhythm-guitar part.

As the rhythm guitar player, you will contribute your unique part to the groove with the rest of the rhythm section. The rhythm guitar part must tap into the groove's rhythmic feel. When you create this part, use rhythms that are being played by the other musicians, too.

LISTEN 5 PLAY

Listen to the bass and guitar playing the groove by themselves. The guitar is simpler than you might expect. This rhythm-guitar part was created to hook up to the other rhythm section parts. Individually, the other parts also sound simple. When all the rhythm-section instruments play together, the groove they create sounds interesting. If all individual parts were too complex, the groove would sound muddy.

HOOKING UP TO ROCK

The way to hook up to a groove is by learning its pulse and rhythmic feel. Then, you will be able to play a rhythm-guitar part that hooks up rhythmically with the rest of the band.

PRACTICE TIP

When you practice rhythms on your guitar, *dampen* the strings with your left hand by lightly resting your fingers over them. Then strum all six strings, flicking your wrist. You should hear a percussive sound, rather than notes. Damping can be used in performance, as well as for practicing rhythms.

LISTEN 3 PLAY

Listen to the first part of "Sweet," and focus on the bass and guitar. As is common in hard rock, the groove in "Sweet" has a clear pulse, and a loud, forceful beat. Notice how the guitar on the recording plays the same rhythm as the bass. The bass line is very prominent in this tune, as it often is in rock. That is one of the reasons why the guitar is so hooked into the groove—because it shares the bass's prominent rhythms.

LISTEN 3 PLAY

Count along with the beat, repeating "1, 2, 3, 4" through every measure. While you count, strum (on dampened strings) along with the snare drum on beats 2 and 4. This is called the *backbeat.* A strong backbeat is one of the characteristics of rock.

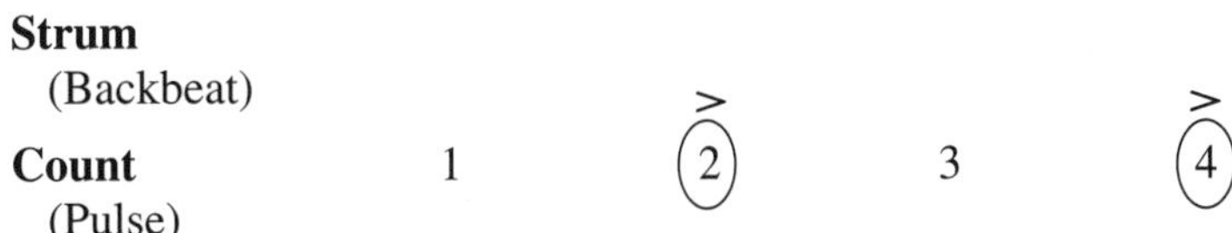

LISTEN 3 PLAY

While you play and count, tap your foot on the quarter-note pulse.

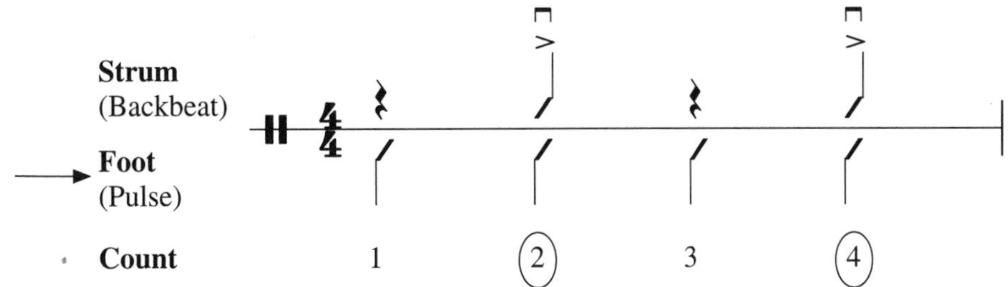

LISTEN 3 PLAY

This tune has a sixteenth-note feel, so change your counting to sixteenth notes, matching the cymbals. On each beat, count evenly, "1 e + a, 2 e + a, 3 e + a, 4 e + a" (say "and" for "+"). Try this first at a slower tempo, without the recording, until you get the hang of it. When you are ready, hook up with the recording.

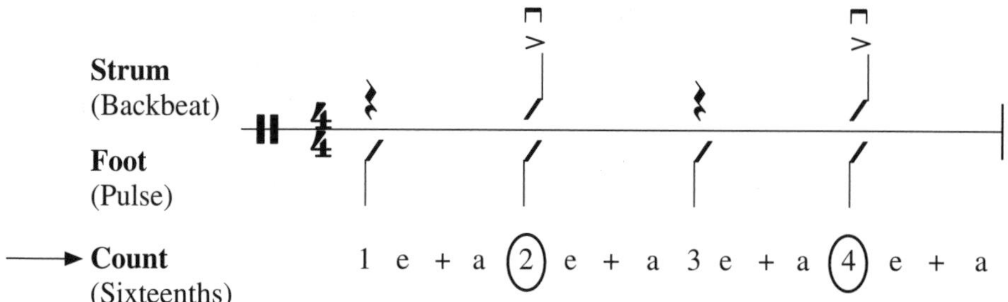

LEARNING "SWEET"

LISTEN 3 PLAY

Play the rhythms of your guitar part. When you are ready, play along with the recording. Hook up with the bass, which plays the same rhythm.

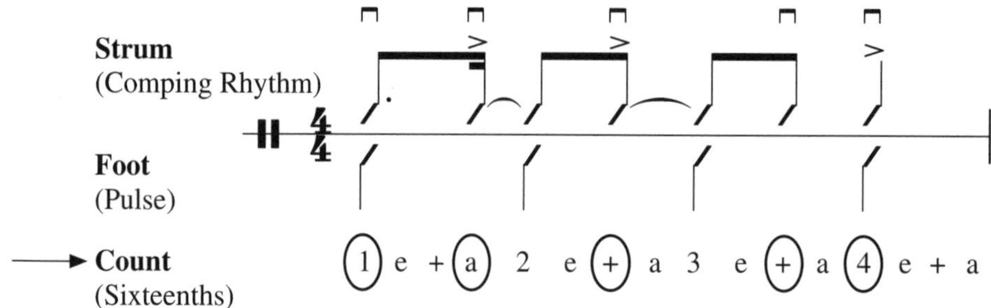

LISTEN 3 PLAY

Play your first part along with the recording, using the written rhythms. Try to count the sixteenth notes as you play.

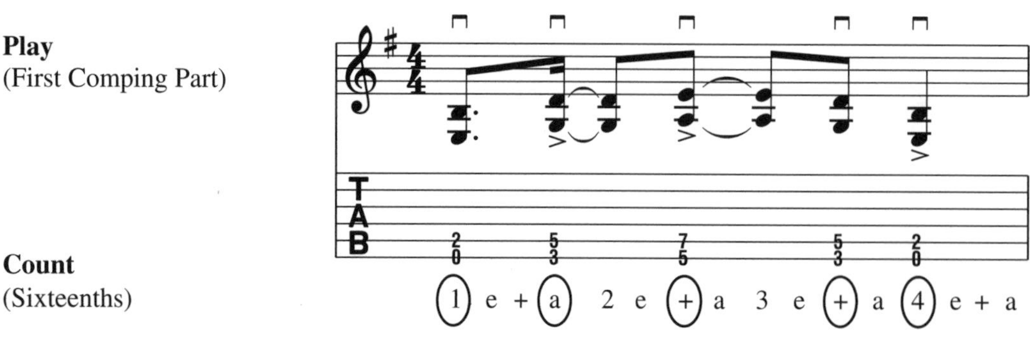

LISTEN 4 PLAY

Listen to the second part to "Sweet," find the pulse, and count along. Then, play the rhythms of your second part. When you are ready, play along with the recording.

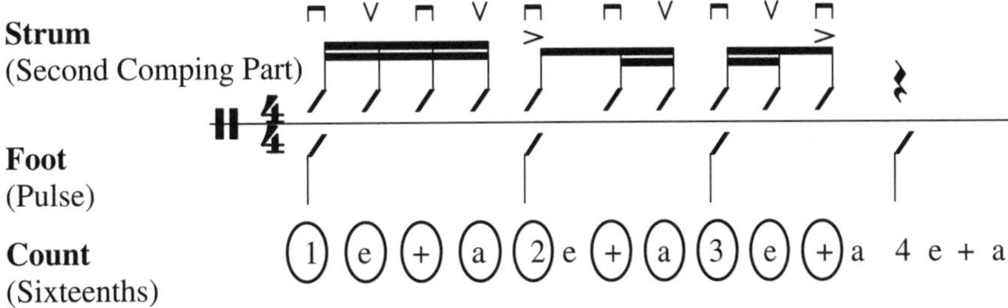

LISTEN 4 PLAY

Play your second comping part using the written rhythms. While you play, count the sixteenths, and hook up with the bass and cymbals.

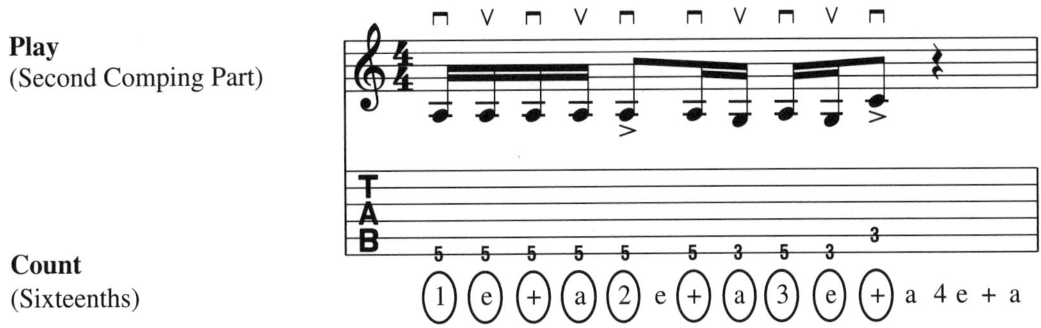

LESSON 3
IMPROVISATION

Improvisation is the invention of a solo. When you improvise, you tell the story of what you think about the tune, and what it means to you. Though an improvised solo may seem spontaneous to the audience, the musician probably did a lot of preparation before performing it. There are two things you must know before you start improvising: when you should play, and what notes will sound good.

FORM AND ARRANGEMENT

When you are preparing to improvise on a tune, start by learning how it is organized. This will let you know when you should start to improvise, and where the chords change.

Listen to "Sweet" and follow the saxophone. After an introduction, the sax plays the melody. Then, it improvises a solo. Finally, it plays the melody again.

During the improvised solo, you can still feel the written melody. That's because the improvisation follows the same chords as the written melody. This repeating chord pattern is the same throughout the entire tune, and is called the song's *form*—its plan or structure.

A common way to show this organization is with a *chord chart*. Chord charts don't show rhythm or pitch, just measures and chord symbols. The slash marks (/ / / /) mean "play in time."

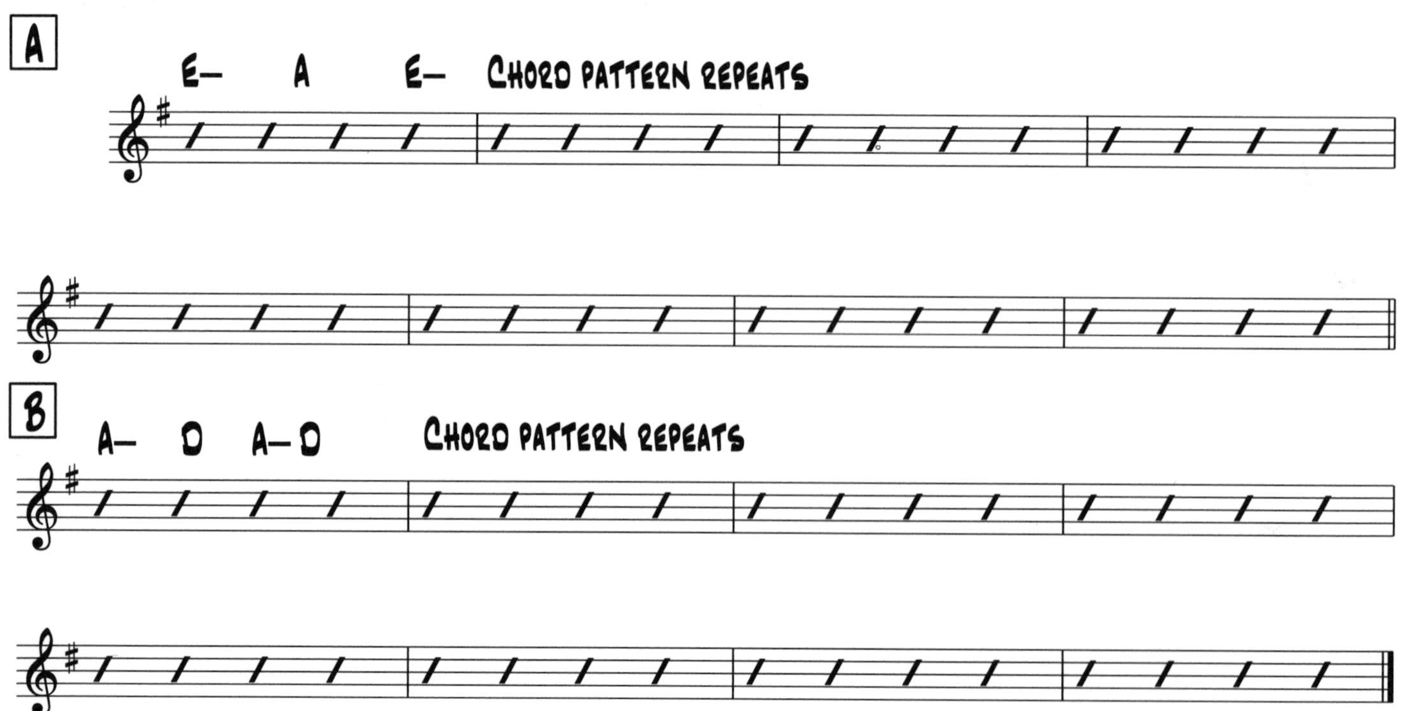

The chord chart makes it easy to see that the form of "Sweet" is sixteen measures long. It has two primary musical ideas: the first eight measures present the first idea (Idea "A"), with the **E– A E–** patterns. The second eight measures present the second idea (Idea "B"), with the **A– D A– D** patterns. This form can be described simply as "AB" or "AB form." These letters help us remember the form, freeing us from having to read while we're performing.

One complete repetition of this form is called a *chorus*. A chorus can feature the written melody, in which case it is called the *head*, or it can feature just the chord structure, supporting an improvisation. (The word *chorus* is also used to mean a song section that is alternated with varying verses. In this book, however, the word "chorus" is only used to mean "once through the form.")

ARRANGING "SWEET"

Your band can choose how many choruses you want to play, and create your own *arrangement* of "Sweet." The number of choruses depends on how many players will improvise when you perform the tune. On the recorded performance of "Sweet," only one player solos (the sax), playing for two choruses. Often, several members of the band will take turns playing choruses of improvised solos. A solo can be one or two choruses, or even more.

On the recording, the same basic arrangement is used for all the tunes: the head, an improvised sax solo, and then the head again. There are often short introductions and endings as well. This is the arrangement for "Sweet" played on the recording:

INTRO	HEAD	SAX SOLO: 2X	HEAD	ENDING
4 MEASURES	1 CHORUS = 16 MEASURES	‖: 1 CHORUS = 16 MEASURES :‖	1 CHORUS = 16 MEASURES	2 MEASURES

When you play "Sweet" with your band, you can play your own arrangement, adding extra solo choruses, different endings, or other changes.

IDEAS FOR IMPROVISING

When you improvise, some notes will sound better than others. There are many ways to find notes that will sound good. You can use the notes from the tune's melody, you can use notes from the chords, and you can use notes from scales that match the tune. Eventually, this becomes intuitive, and you can just follow your ear.

Pentatonic Scales

The sax soloist on this recording of "Sweet" built much of his solo using notes from a *pentatonic scale*. Pentatonic scales are among the simplest and most versatile types of scales in all of music. All pentatonic scales have five notes. There are two common types of pentatonic scales: major and minor. For "Sweet," the soloist used the *minor pentatonic scale* built on E. This scale works well here because the tune is in E minor.

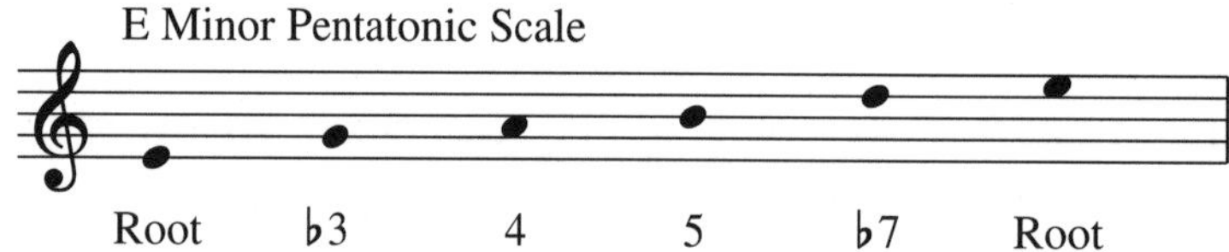

The magic of the minor pentatonic scale is that nearly any series or combination of its notes sounds musically pleasing. It is easy to improvise pentatonic *licks* (short melodic figures or phrases) that sound good.

When you solo, you will want to use notes in more than just one octave, so practice the notes of the E minor pentatonic scale in the following range, using the fingering shown.

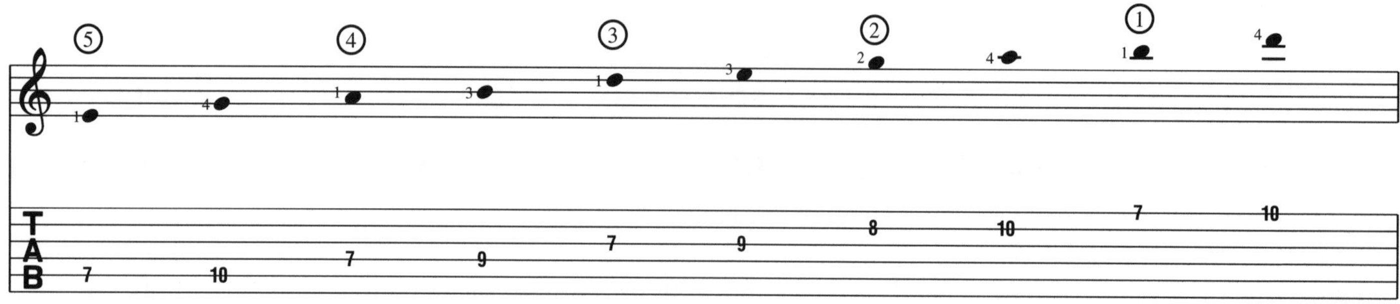

CALL AND RESPONSE

Echo

Listen to each phrase, and then play it back, echoing it exactly. Each two-bar phrase comes from the E minor pentatonic scale. Play just the melody, using one hand. Follow the form and try to capture each phrase's rhythms. Slashes ("/") in measures marked "play" mean that you should play during those measures. Listen carefully, and hook up with the groove.

LISTEN 6 PLAY

Keep practicing that track until you can echo all phrases perfectly. Then do the same thing for the phrases on this next track.

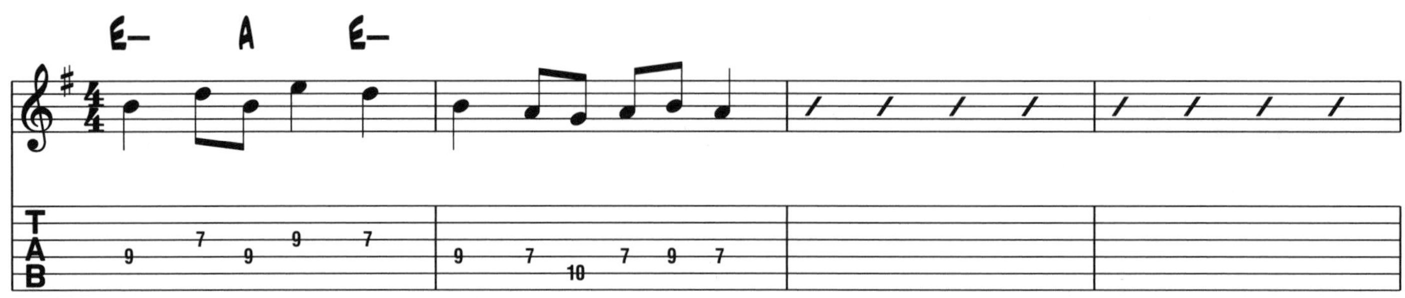

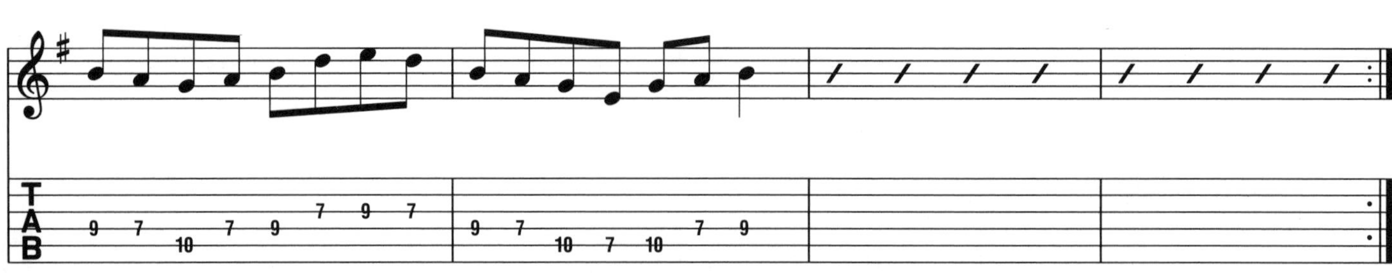

Answer

LISTEN 6,7 PLAY

Play the same two tracks again. This time, instead of echoing the phrases exactly, answer them with your own improvised phrases. Imitate the sound and rhythmic feel of the phrases you hear, and only use notes of the E minor pentatonic scale.

Write out some of your own two-measure phrases, like the ones you have been playing. Don't worry about perfecting your notation; just sketch out your ideas. This will help you remember them when you are improvising.

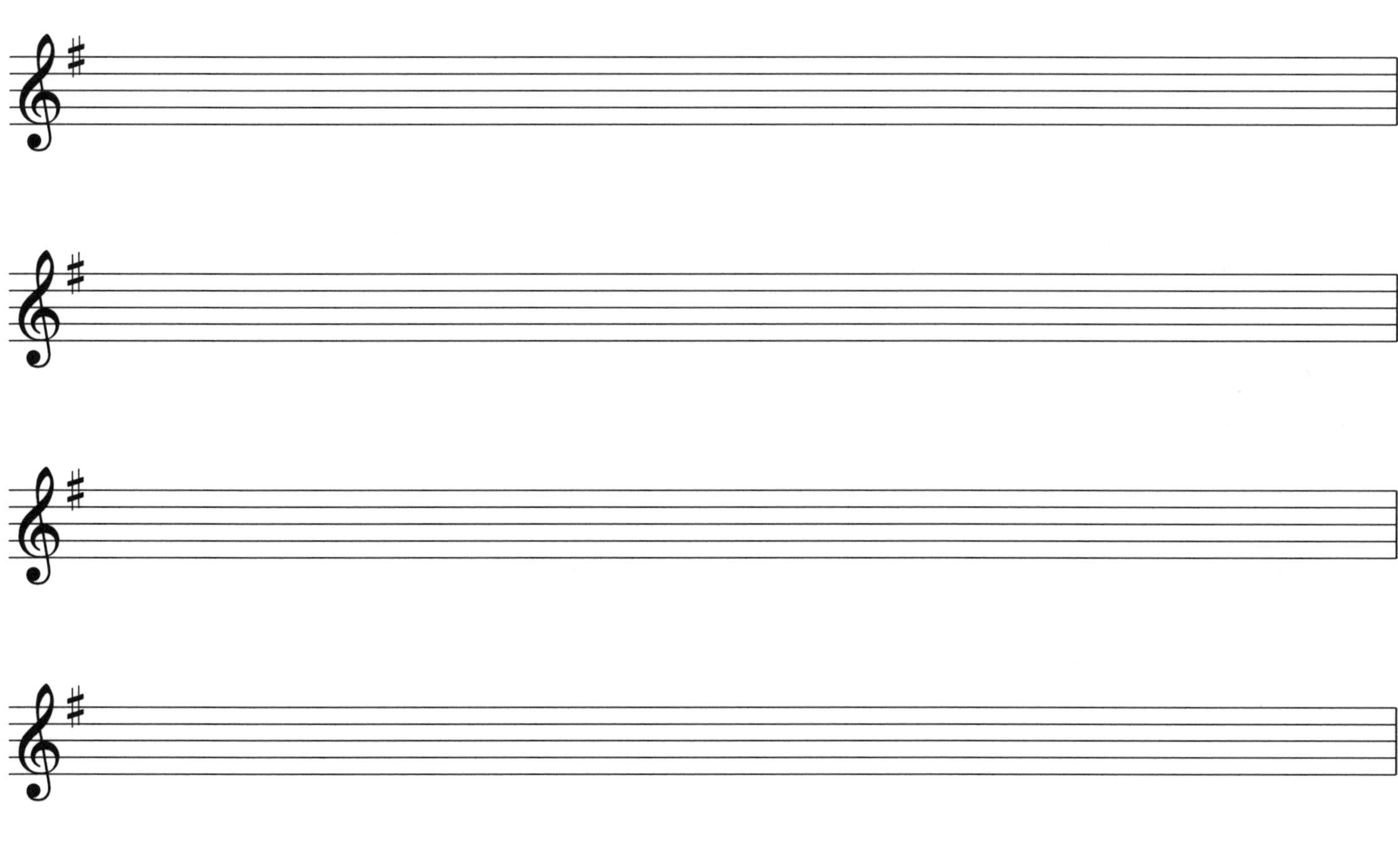

LISTEN 8 PLAY

Create a one-chorus solo using any techniques you have learned. Memorize your solo and practice it along with the recording.

> **PLAY IN A BAND TIP**
>
> When playing in a band, listen to the other players' parts and try to create a musical conversation. This makes playing much more fun, and more musical too. When you are improvising a solo, listen to what the other instruments are playing. They will suggest many ideas that you can use in your solo, and you will inspire each other.

LESSON 4
READING

When you play in a band, sometimes you will get a guitar part for the tune that shows exactly what you should play. Other times, you will get a lead sheet, giving you more freedom to create your own part. You should be able to play from either one.

GUITAR PART

Read the written guitar part to "Sweet." Above the guitar part is a smaller staff that shows the melody and chord symbols. Some guitar parts show the melody, but often they do not. Notice that there is no tablature under the guitar part. Tab is mostly used in song books and in teaching methods, but very rarely on actual gigs. Practice reading regular notation. That is what you will see most often.

Intro	Introduction. The written part begins with an introduction, which is made up of four measures of the B section.
Hard Rock	Style indication. This tune is hard rock, and you should play it in that style: prominent guitar, strong beat, sixteenth-note feel, and other elements typical of that hard-edged sound.
♩ = 86	Metronome marking. This tells you how fast you should play this tune. If you have a metronome, set it to 86, and play "Sweet" at that tempo.
𝄆 𝄇	Repeat signs. Play the music between these signs twice (or more).
[A]	Rehearsal letter. These are different than form letters, which you saw in lesson 3. These letters help you when you are practicing with other musicians because everyone's parts have the same letters marked at the same places.
[A9]	Rehearsal letter with measure number. These mark different areas within a chorus. Again, this can be helpful during rehearsals.

After solos, Repeat to Ending

When the soloists are finished, play the head one more time, and then proceed to the measures marked "Ending."

Ending	A final section that is added to the form. End the tune with these measures.

Play along with the recording of "Sweet," following the notated guitar part exactly. This part is typical of a guitar part that you might create for "Sweet."

Sweet

Guitar Part

By Matt Marvuglio

"Hard Rock" ♩ = 86

Intro

A– D A– D

Melody

Guitar

A

E– A E–

A9

A– D A– D

After solos, repeat to ending

Ending

E– A E–

LEAD SHEET

Lead sheets present the chords and melody, written in treble clef. Lead sheets give you more interpretive freedom than full guitar parts do. Notice that there is no written introduction on this lead sheet. The introduction you hear in the recording is an interpretation of the lead sheet by that band. Your band should create your own unique arrangement.

Play "Sweet" and follow the lead sheet. When you play a rhythm-guitar part, try varying the rhythms, or even the specific chord notes you choose.

Sweet

By Matt Marvuglio

"Hard Rock" ♩ = 86

E– A E–

A– D A– D

Ending

PLAY IN A BAND TIP

While you play, follow the lead sheet. It will help you keep your place in the form.

CHAPTER I
DAILY PRACTICE ROUTINE

PICKING PRACTICE

Practice downstrokes. Finish each stroke by resting the pick on the next string (on the high E string, stop one string's distance away).

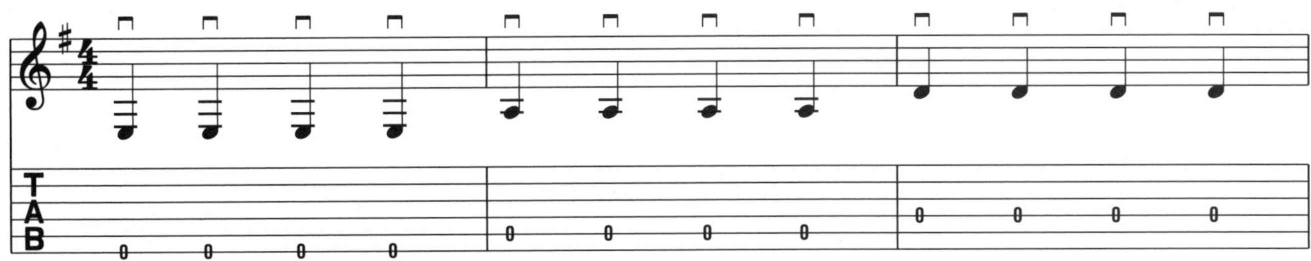

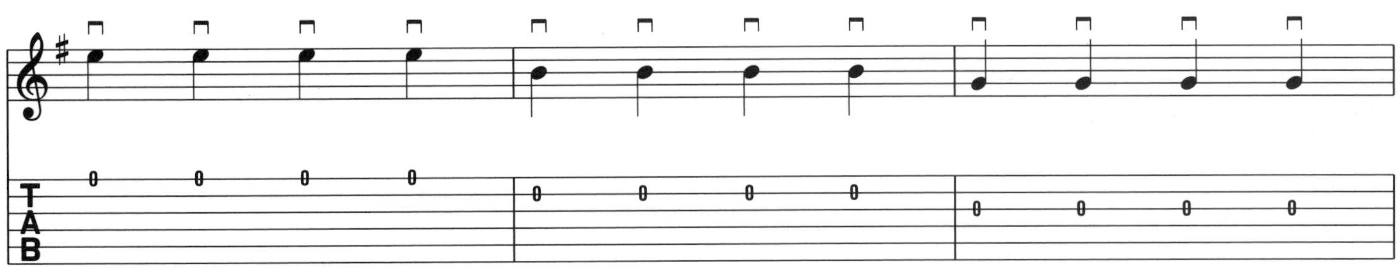

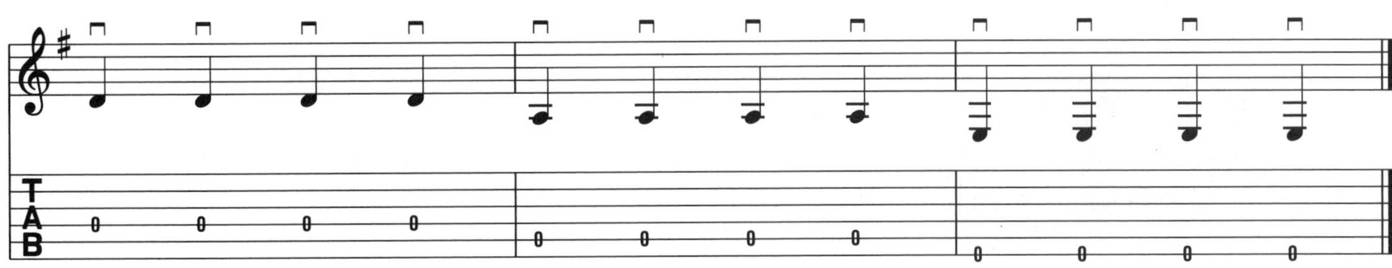

ALTERNATE PICKING PRACTICE

Practice alternate picking (mixing upstrokes and downstrokes), playing the rhythms of the first lick to "Sweet."

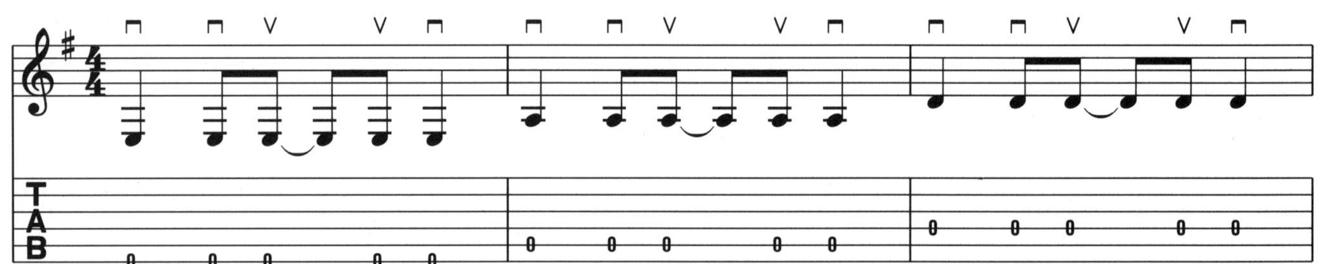

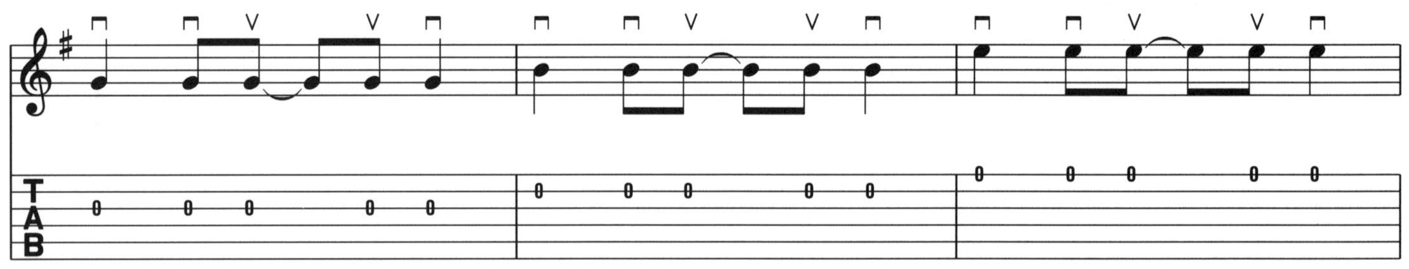

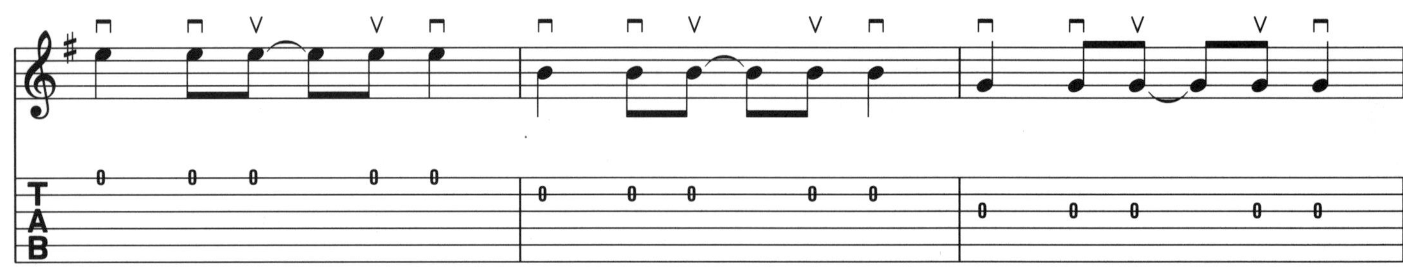

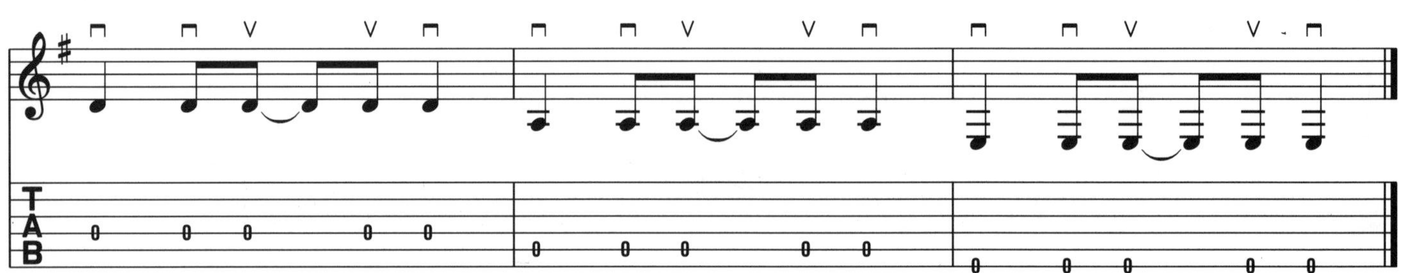

PRACTICE TIP

Alternate picking allows you to play notes very quickly. The motion is "all in the wrist" of the right hand. Move just enough to play the note, with no wasted motion.

MEMORIZE

LISTEN 8 PLAY

Memorizing the licks and melodies from these exercises will help you play the tune, especially when you improvise. What you practice helps you when you perform. But performing is the best practice, so get together with other musicians and learn these tunes with your own band.

Memorize the guitar part to "Sweet." Also memorize the lead sheet. The "Summary" shows everything you need to play "Sweet" from a lead sheet. Memorizing it will help you memorize the tune.

PRACTICE TIP

Write out a chord chart for "Sweet" by memory. This is a good way to help memorize tunes, and you can do it anywhere or any time. Don't worry about making it neat; just sketch out the measures and the chords, and think about solo ideas you might play over them.

SUMMARY
FORM
16-BAR AB
(1 CHORUS = 16 BARS)
A: 8 M.
B: 8 M.
ARRANGEMENT
INTRO: 4 M.
1 CHORUS MELODY
2 CHORUS SOLO
1 CHORUS MELODY
END: 2 M.
HARMONY
A E– A B A– D
SCALE
E MINOR PENTATONIC

PLAY "SWEET" WITH YOUR OWN BAND!

PLAYING BLUES — CHAPTER II

"Do It Now" is a *blues* tune. Blues began in the late 1800s, and it has had a profound influence on American music styles, including rock, jazz, and soul. To hear more blues, listen to artists such as B.B. King, the Blues Brothers, Robben Ford, Bonnie Raitt, James Cotton, Albert King, and Paul Butterfield.

LESSON 5
TECHNIQUE/THEORY

Listen to "Do It Now" on the recording. In this tune, the guitar plays the melody during the head and chords during the solo.

Here is the melody:

Here are the chord patterns:

First Part **Second Part** **Third Part** **First Part (repeats)**

Play along with the recording and try to match the rhythms you hear. You can play just the top note of each chord, for now.

CHORDS AND COMPING

On the recording, the rhythm-guitar player accompanies the sax soloist with *chords* (three or more notes sounded together). In chapter 1, you learned to play power chords, which have only two notes. All other chords have three notes or more.

Accompanying a soloist with chords is called *comping*. Guitars and keyboards often play comping parts in grooves, though sometimes, they play melody or double a bass riff instead.

"Do It Now" is in the key of F. Here is the written notation and chord frame for a full F major chord. Try it:

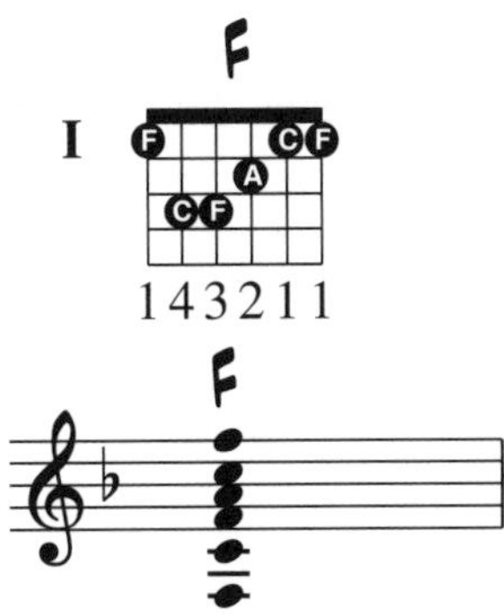

Usually, you won't need to play all these notes—especially when you're playing in a band, and the keyboardist is also playing chords. A simpler way to play an F chord is to stick to the basics, and play a smaller *chord form* (arrangement of chord notes). Play this chord form and notice how its sound compares to the larger form of the F chord you just played:

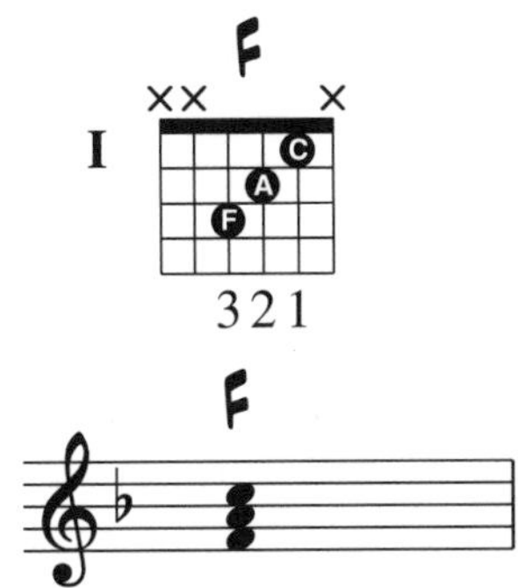

In "Do It Now," you'll also be playing the B♭ major chord. Here is the form you'll play on the first chord pattern:

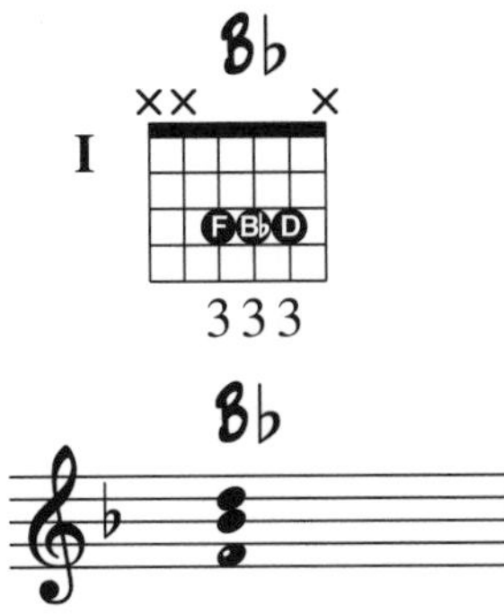

Listen to the guitar chord rhythms in "Do It Now" and play the first chord pattern in time with the first four measures. You'll learn chord forms for other comping patterns in the Daily Practice Routine.

LISTEN 10 PLAY

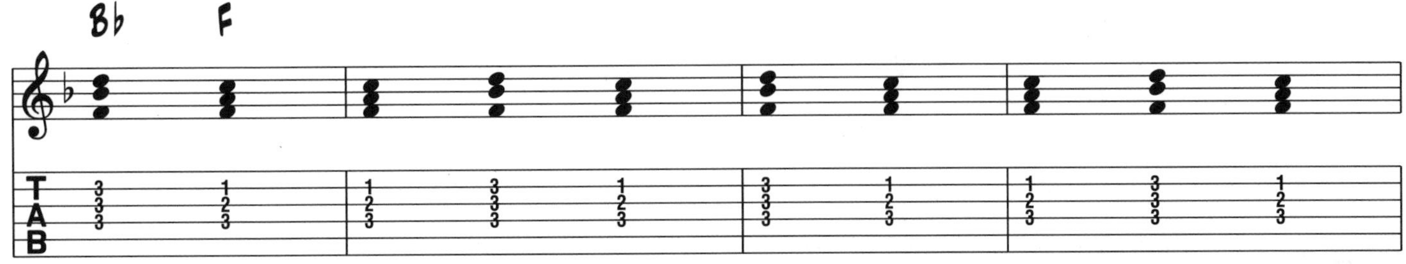

LESSON 6
LEARNING THE GROOVE

HOOKING UP TO A BLUES SHUFFLE

LISTEN 9 PLAY

Listen to "Do It Now." This groove has its roots in traditional r&b, gospel, and jazz. The feel is often called a *12/8 shuffle* because of the twelve eighth notes in each bar. (The drums play these on the ride cymbal or hi-hat.)

Tap your foot on every beat, and count triplets: "1 trip-let 2 trip-let 3 trip-let 4 trip-let." The basic pulse (tap) is on the quarter note. However, each pulse also has an underlying triplet that divides the beat into three equal parts. Play the triplets on dampened strings.

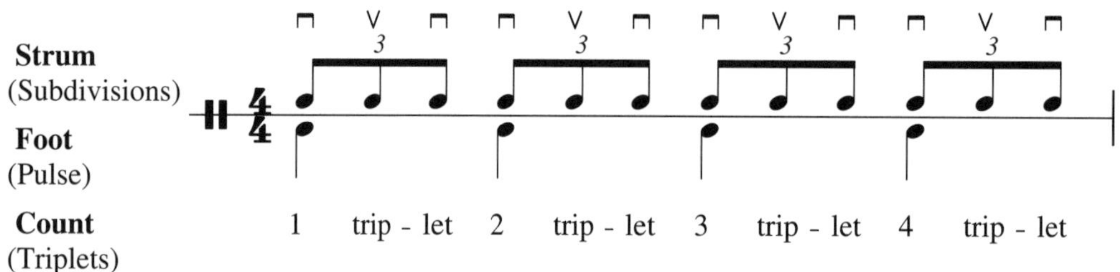

This triplet feel is part of what makes the beat a *shuffle*. While all shuffles don't include triplets on every single beat, the underlying triplet *feel* is always present.

The triplet is a fundamental aspect of all swing and shuffle beats. Understanding and feeling the concept of "subdivisions" (dividing the pulse into smaller rhythms) will help you play many other kinds of grooves.

LEARNING "DO IT NOW"

LISTEN 9 PLAY

Listen to "Do It Now." Find the pulse, and play dampened strings along with the backbeat (beats 2 and 4):

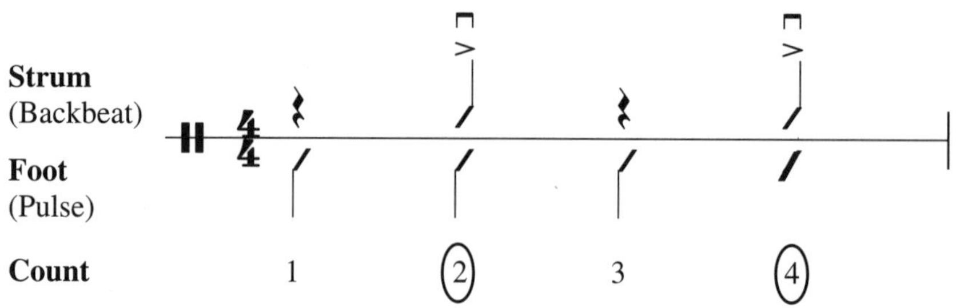

Count triplets on each beat, as you strum on the backbeat. When you are ready, do this along with the recording. The hi-hat matches your counting.

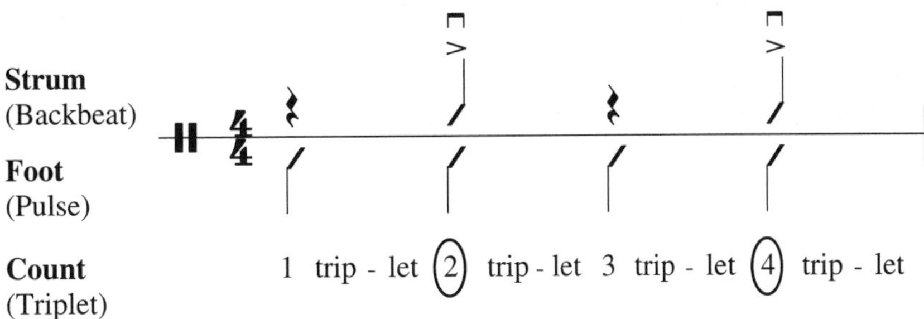

Play the rhythms of your comping part. When you are ready, play along with the recording. Every other measure, you will hook up with the hi-hat on the "let" of beat 2's triplet.

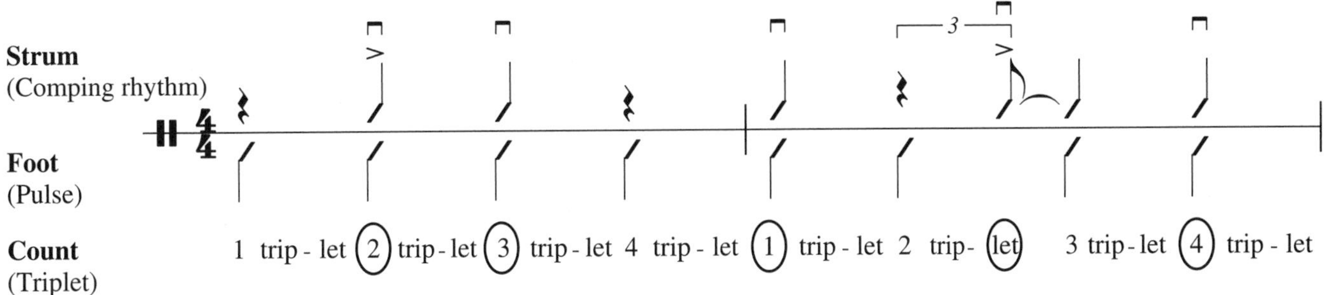

PERFORMANCE TIP

The keyboard, who is playing a similar comping part, plays different rhythms during the head and during the solo. That's because the guitar plays the melody during the head, but adds its own comping part during the solo section. When more than one instrument is comping, they often play different rhythms so that their parts fit together and do not interfere with each other.

LISTEN 9 PLAY

Play your comping part along with the recording, using the written rhythms. Count the triplets while you play. The first comping pattern is given below. The second comping pattern is similar, but uses different chords. Use your ear to figure out the second and third comping patterns.

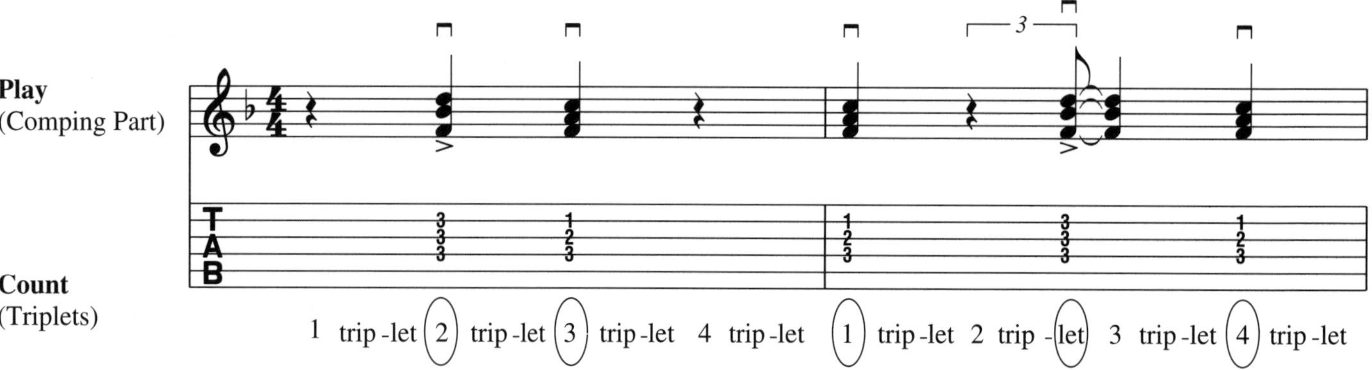

LISTEN 11 PLAY

Play the melody along with the recording. Count triplets as you play.

SWING EIGHTH NOTES

Eighth notes in shuffle grooves are usually played as triplets, even though they are notated as *straight* eighth notes.

Straight **Swing**

Though these rhythms look different, in some musical styles, they are played the same. Eighth notes that are played as triplets are called *swing eighth notes*. Swing eighth notes are common in many styles of music, including blues, jazz, and swing. Sometimes, the word "swing," "swing feel," or "shuffle" will appear on the lead sheet telling you how to play the eighth notes.

On the lead sheet, the melody to "Do It Now" shows eighth notes notated like this:

Written:

Since it is a shuffle tune, they are played like this:

Played:

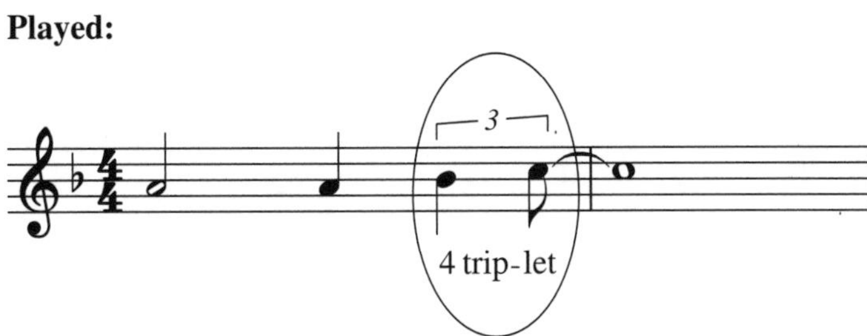

Notating triplets as straight eighths is very common in shuffle grooves.

LESSON 7
IMPROVISATION

FORM AND ARRANGEMENT: 12-BAR BLUES FORM

LISTEN 9 PLAY

Listen to "Do It Now" and follow the form. The form of "Do It Now" is a *12-bar blues.* Its form is twelve measures long, with chords organized in this sequence:

A 12-bar blues has three 4-bar phrases. It is common for the first two phrases in the melody to be similar and the third one to be different. This form is very common in many styles of music, including jazz, rock, and funk.

Notice how the first two phrases of the melody are similar:

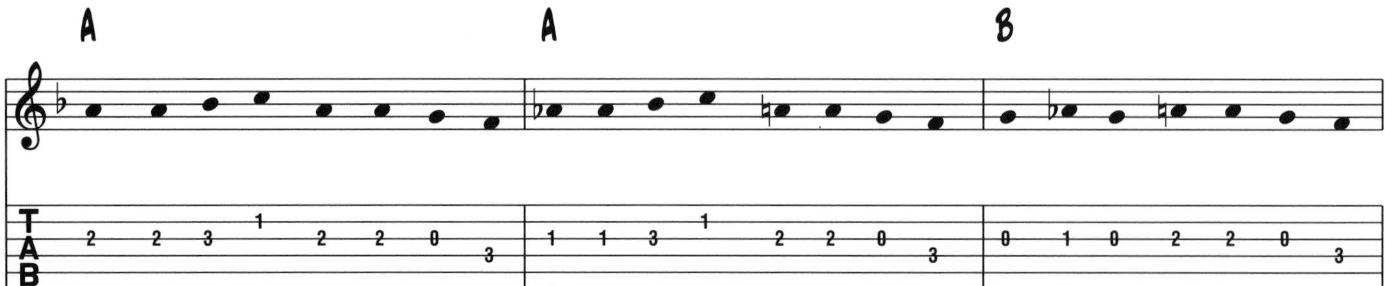

LISTEN 9 PLAY

Listen to "Do It Now" and follow the arrangement. How many times does the form repeat at the head? How many times does it repeat during the solo? Why does the soloist play higher in the second chorus of the solo?

ARRANGEMENT

"Do It Now" begins with the drum playing two beats of triplets. This is called a *pickup*—a short introduction, less than a measure long, that leads to a strong downbeat. The arrangement played on the recording is:

Pickup	Head: 2x	Sax Solo: 2x	Head	Ending
2 Beats Drums	‖: 1 Chorus = 12 Measures :‖	‖: 1 Chorus = 12 Measures :‖	1 Chorus = 12 Measures	4 Measures

PRACTICE TIP

When you listen to any music, figure out the arrangement. How long is the head? Is there an introduction or an ending? How many solo choruses does the band take?

BLUES SCALE

In chapter 1, you learned to improvise using the minor pentatonic scale. Here is the F minor pentatonic scale:

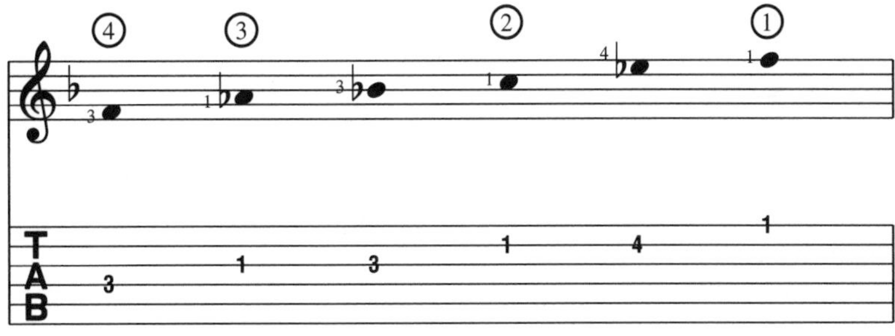

The F *blues scale* has just one more note—the flat fifth degree (C-flat or B-natural):

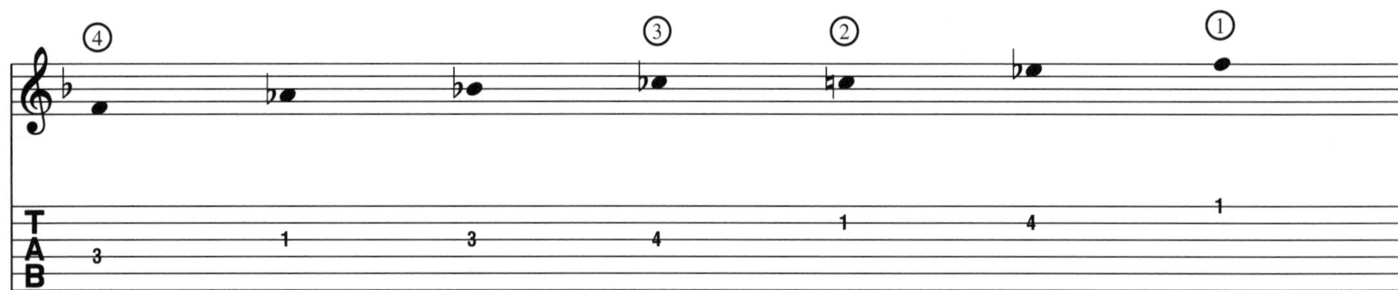

Here it is an octave higher:

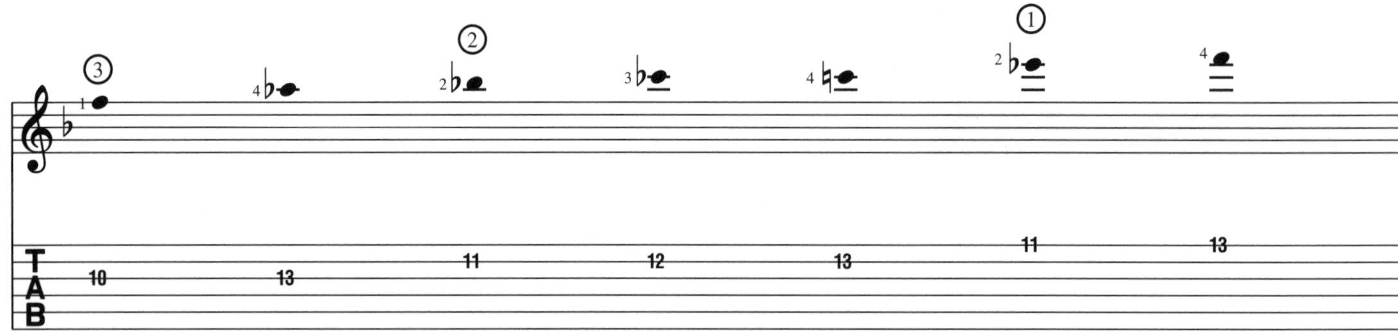

This scale can be used to improvise over all chords of "Do It Now." There is one note in the melody that is not in this scale: A-natural. You can use A-natural in your improvisation, as well. One cool thing about the blues scale is that you can play with it, adding a special note or two to make it work better for a tune. Adding an A-natural here is a good variation to try.

CALL AND RESPONSE

1. Echo each phrase, exactly as you hear it.
2. Improvise an answer to each phrase. Imitate the sound and rhythmic feel of the phrase you hear, and use the notes from the F blues scale.

LISTEN 13 PLAY

Listen

Play

F7

Bb7

F7

C7

Bb7

F7

Write out a few of your own ideas. Use notes from the F blues scale.

LISTEN 14 PLAY

Create a solo using any techniques you have played. Memorize your solo, and practice it along with the recording.

LESSON 8
READING

GUITAR PART

This *chart* (written part) uses symbols and instructions that direct you to skip around the pages. When you get the hang of these symbols, you will see that they help reduce the number of written measures, and make the chart easier to read quickly, at a glance. Sometimes, these directions are called the chart's *road map*.

2 BEATS DRUMS Pickup. Short introduction (less than a measure).

𝄋 Sign. Later, there will be a direction (D.S., or "from the sign") telling you to jump to this symbol from another location in the music.

𝄌 Coda symbol. "Coda" is another word for "ending." On the last chorus, skip from the first coda symbol to the second coda symbol (at the end of the piece). This symbol may also have the words "To Coda," or other directions (such as "last time only"). Often, you will just see the coda symbol by itself.

D.S. AL 𝄌 From the sign (𝄋), and take the coda. Jump back to the sign (first measure, after the pickup), and play from there. When you reach the first coda symbol, skip ahead to the next coda symbol (at the end).

AFTER SOLOS When all solo choruses are finished, follow this direction.

B Different choruses may be marked with different letters. In this tune, the head is marked "A," and the improvisation choruses are marked "B."

SOLO Solo chorus. Play this part when other musicians in the band improvise. When you play this tune with your own band, you might repeat this section several times, depending on how many people solo. When you solo, then obviously, you won't play this written part.

Play the written guitar part along with the recording. Remember to swing your eighth notes.

LISTEN 14 PLAY

Do It Now

Guitar Part

By Matt Marvuglio

B
SOLOS
F7
Bb7
F7
C7
Bb7
F7
AFTER SOLOS, D.S. AL
CODA
C7
Bb7
F7

LEAD SHEET

Play "Do It Now" and follow the lead sheet. Play the melody at the head and your own comping part during the solos.

LISTEN 14 PLAY

Do It Now

By Matt Marvuglio

"Medium Shuffle" ♩ = 96

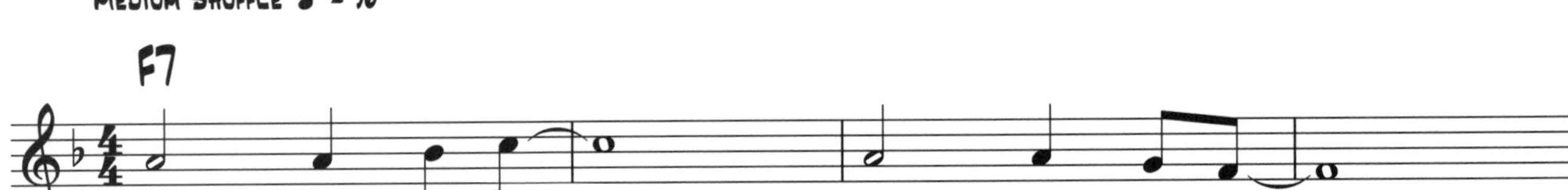

CHAPTER II
DAILY PRACTICE ROUTINE

STRUMMING CHORDS

The easiest chord to strum on a guitar is a G triad played on the second, third, and fourth open strings:

Here's how to strum this chord:

1. Place the pick on the fourth string.
2. Glide the pick down, over strings two, three, and four, until your pick rests on the first string. All three strings should sound simultaneously, not as three separate notes.
3. Go right back to the fourth string and strum it again.

Strum this G triad in steady time, once per beat. Practice strumming without looking at the strings. Close your eyes, move your hand away from your guitar, and then find the strings by feel, keeping your eyes closed.

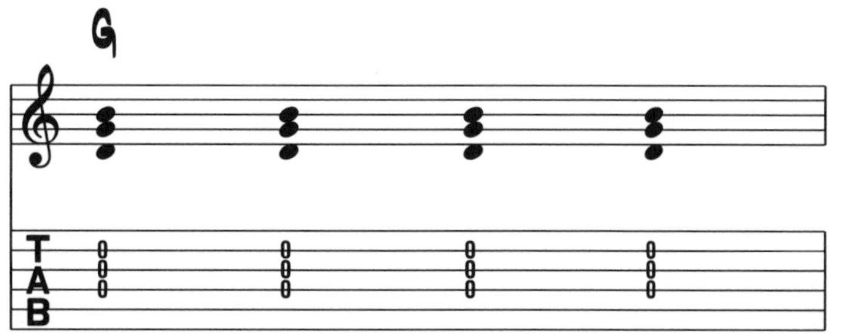

BARRE CHORDS

Hold your first finger flat against third fret, on just the second, third, and fourth strings. This is the fingering for one of the B♭ chords used in "Do It Now." When one finger holds down several strings on the same fret, it is called a *barre* (or *bar*) *chord*.

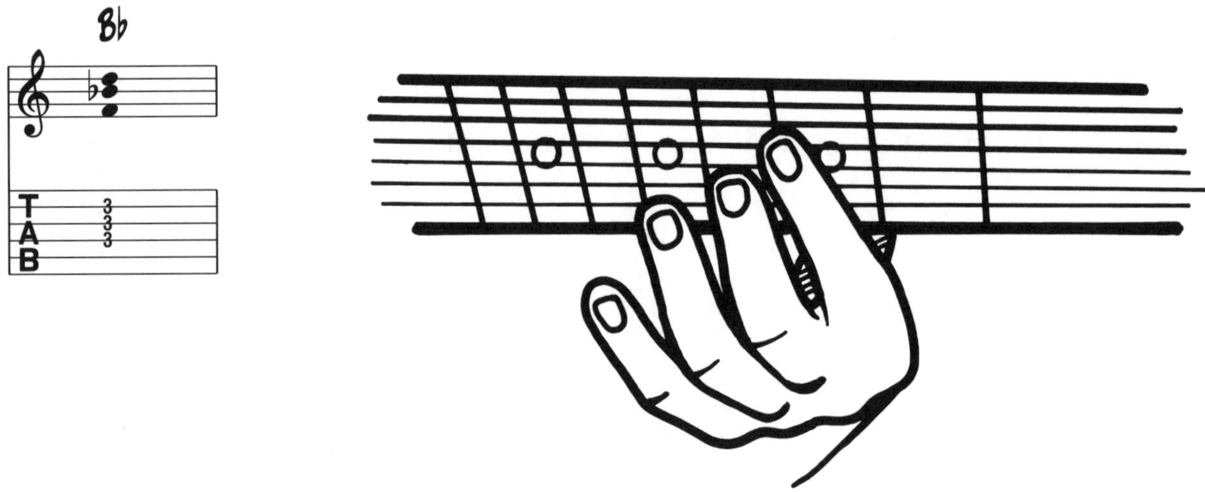

This is almost exactly what you did to create the G chord. You can move your finger "bar" to any fret. Congratulations, you can now play more than a dozen chords on the guitar!

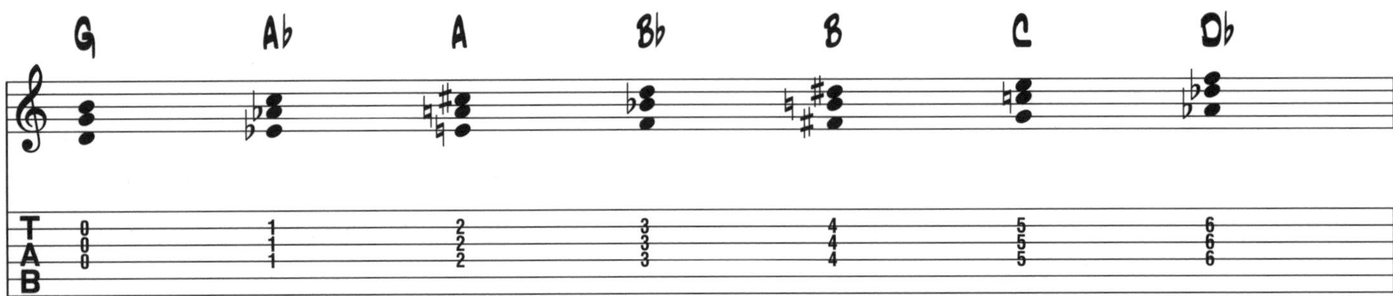

Keep going! This is one of the great things about the guitar: the same hand position can be used on different frets to play many different chords.

PRACTICE TIP

Practice going up the fretboard with these barre chords *without looking at the guitar.* Close your eyes, and memorize how it feels to play them.

CHORD FORMS FOR "DO IT NOW"

"Do It Now" has six chord forms, all played on the second, third, and fourth strings. Notice that there are two different forms of the B♭ chord—the second, placing the F in the higher octave. Also notice that some of these chord forms don't include the chord's root. When you play in a band, the root will be played by the bass, and maybe the keyboards or others, so you don't always need to play it.

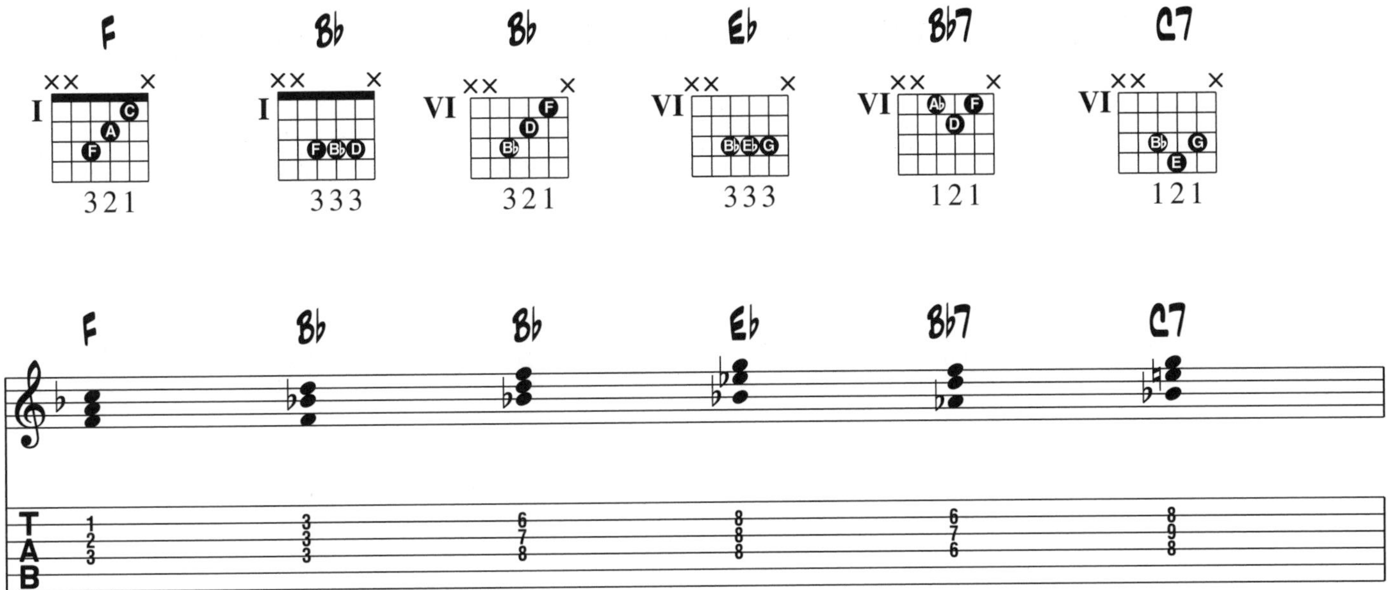

Play these chords along with the recording. Practice switching between chords as smoothly as you can, keeping steady time. You may prefer to practice your part away from the recording first, starting at a slow tempo and gradually increasing the speed as you become more comfortable playing these chords.

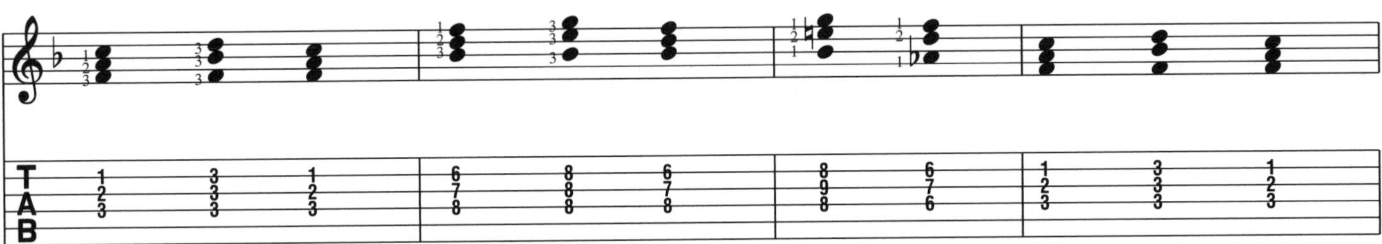

COMPING PRACTICE

Here is the comping part played by the guitar. Play it along with the recording.

LISTEN 14 PLAY

F7

B♭7 F7

C7 B♭7 F7

Here is the keyboard's comping part. Try this one too:

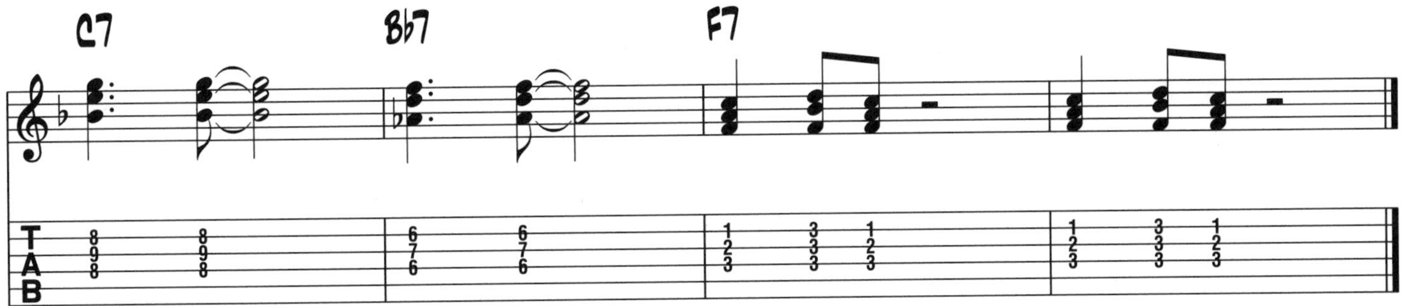

Listen to the recording, and notice how the guitar and keyboards hook up their comping parts, each playing different parts of the rhythm.

SOLO PRACTICE

Play this solo to "Do It Now" along with the recording. Then create your own solo using notes from the F blues scale. Write down a few of your ideas.

LISTEN 14 PLAY

MEMORIZE

LISTEN 14 PLAY

Create a comping part and a solo using any techniques you have learned. Memorize your part, and then play through the tune with the recording as if you were performing it live. Keep your place in the form, and don't stop, whatever happens.

> **PERFORMANCE TIP**
>
> If you make a mistake or get lost, keep your composure, and pretend that everything is going fine. Listen to the other instruments, hear what chords they are playing, and find your way back into the form. You can even practice getting lost and then finding your place. Start the recording at a random point within the track, and then follow your ear.

SUMMARY

FORM
12-Bar Blues
(1 chorus = 12 bars)

ARRANGEMENT
Pickup: 2 Beats Drums
2 Chorus Melody
2 Chorus Solo
1 Chorus Melody
End: 4 m.

HARMONY
F7 B♭7 C7

SCALE
F Blues

PLAY "DO IT NOW" WITH YOUR OWN BAND!

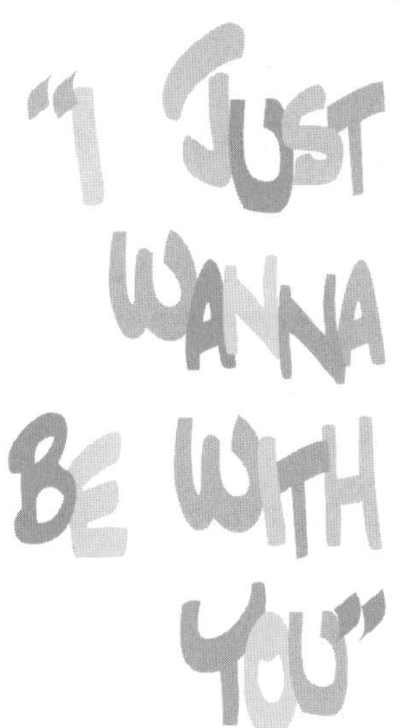

"I Just Wanna Be With You" is a *blues swing. Swing* is a dance-oriented, big-band style from the 1930s. To hear more swing, listen to artists such as Count Basie, Benny Goodman, the Squirrel Nut Zippers, Diana Krall, Branford Marsalis, Kevin Eubanks, Joanne Brackeen, Cherry Poppin' Daddies, and Big Bad Voodoo Daddy.

LESSON 9
TECHNIQUE/THEORY

Play "I Just Wanna Be With You" along with the recording. This tune is a minor blues, similar to "Do It Now."

LISTEN 15 PLAY

First, the guitar plays melody with the saxophone:

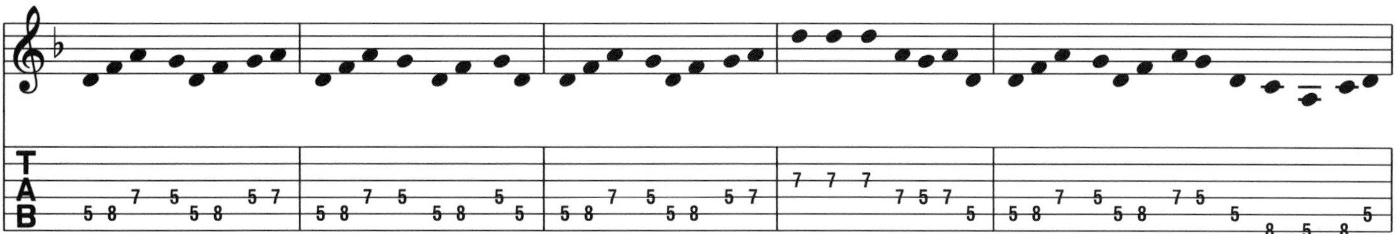

During the solo, the guitar comps using these chord patterns:

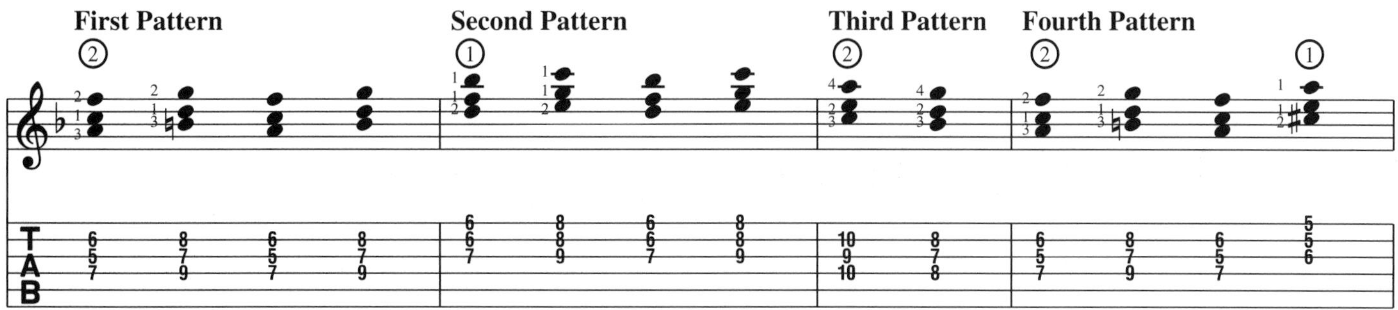

LESSON 10
LEARNING THE GROOVE

LISTEN 15 PLAY

Listen to "I Just Wanna Be With You" and focus on the cymbals. This tune is a shuffle, like "Do It Now.' There is a triplet feel under each beat. The main difference is that in this tune, the middle triplet of each beat is left out. This is common in swing.

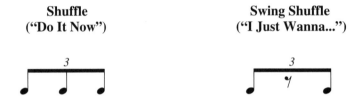

This syncopated "push-pull" feel is basic to jazz and r&b. Sometimes this feel is called a "double shuffle" because the drummer plays the same rhythm with both hands. In swing, the bass player usually plays a "walking" quarter-note bass line.

HOOKING UP TO SWING

LISTEN 15 PLAY

Listen to "I Just Wanna Be With You." Find the beat, and play along with the backbeat:

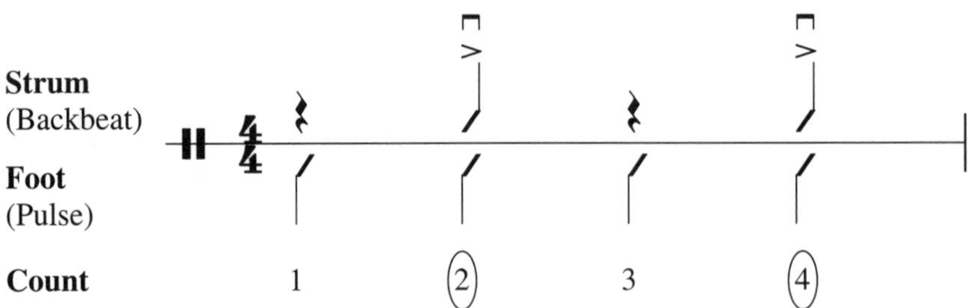

This tune has a swing feel, so count triplets on each beat as you play along with the backbeat. When you are ready, do this along with the recording. The hi-hat matches your counting.

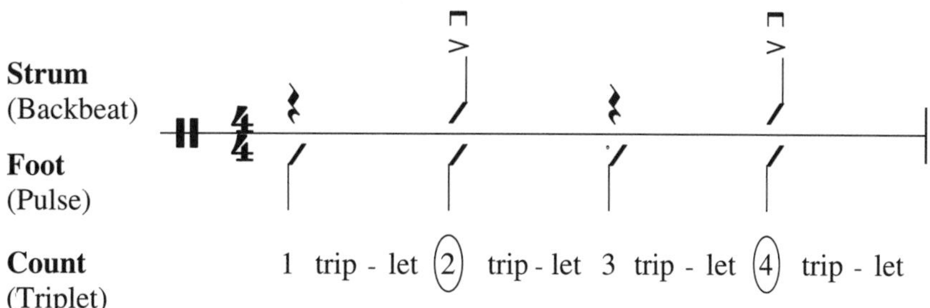

Play swing eighth notes, which you learned in chapter 2.

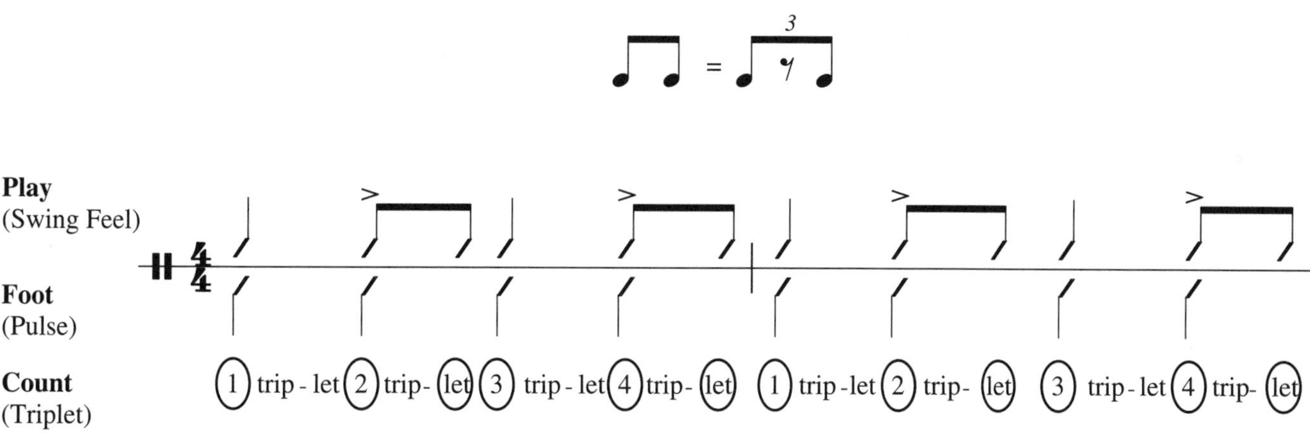

LEARNING "I JUST WANNA BE WITH YOU"

LISTEN 15 PLAY

Strum the actual rhythms of your part. When you are ready, play along with the recording.

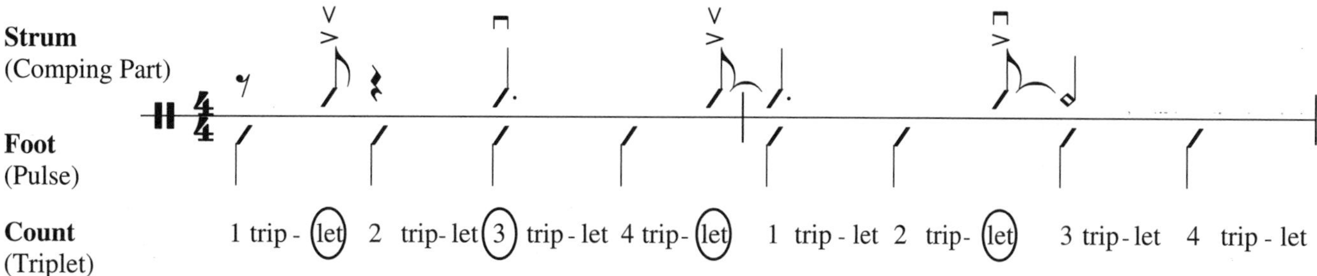

SYNCOPATION

The final note of the first measure is accented. Notes on beat 4 are usually not stressed, so this comes as a surprise—an interruption of the expected pulse. A rhythm such as this is called a *syncopation.*

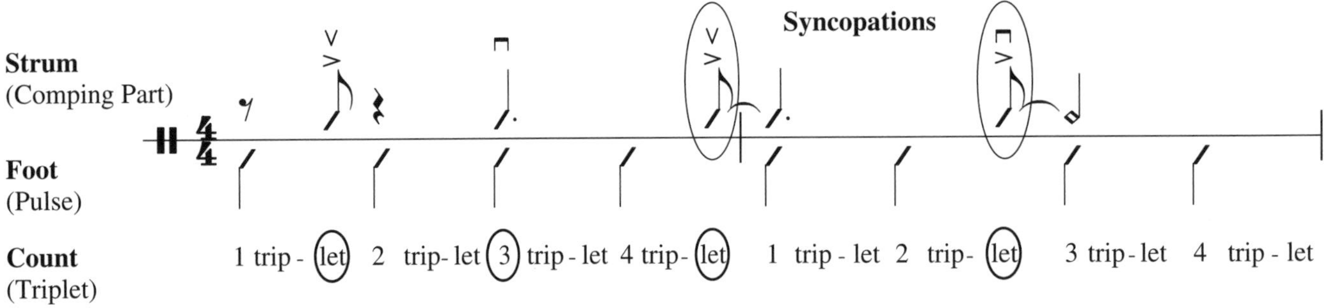

LISTEN 15 PLAY

Play your comping part using the written rhythms. While you play, count the triplets and accent the syncopation.

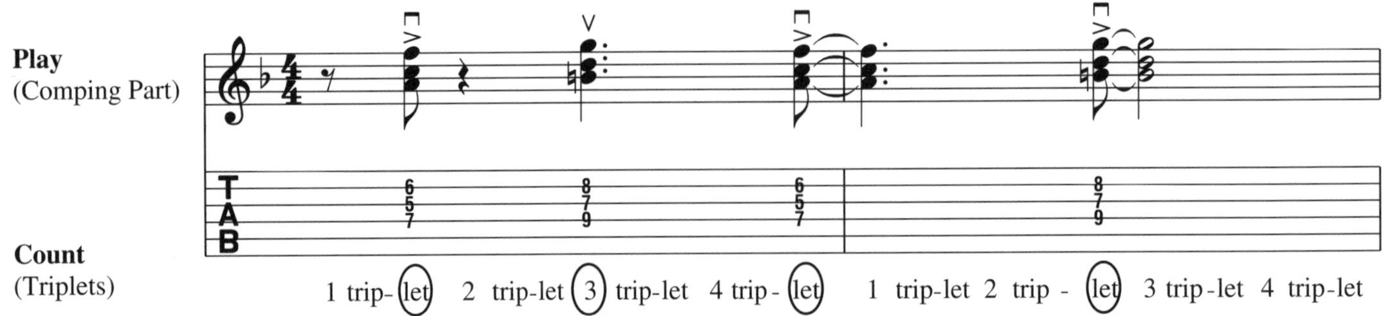

PRACTICE TIP

Practice slowly. Before you can play something fast, you must be able to play it slowly. Know where your fingers are going before you move them, and try to hear the notes in your head before you play them.

LESSON 11
IMPROVISATION

FORM AND ARRANGEMENT

LISTEN 15 PLAY

Listen to "I Just Wanna Be With You" and follow the form. This tune is another 12-bar blues. The form of each chorus is twelve measures long and divided into three phrases, just like "Do It Now."

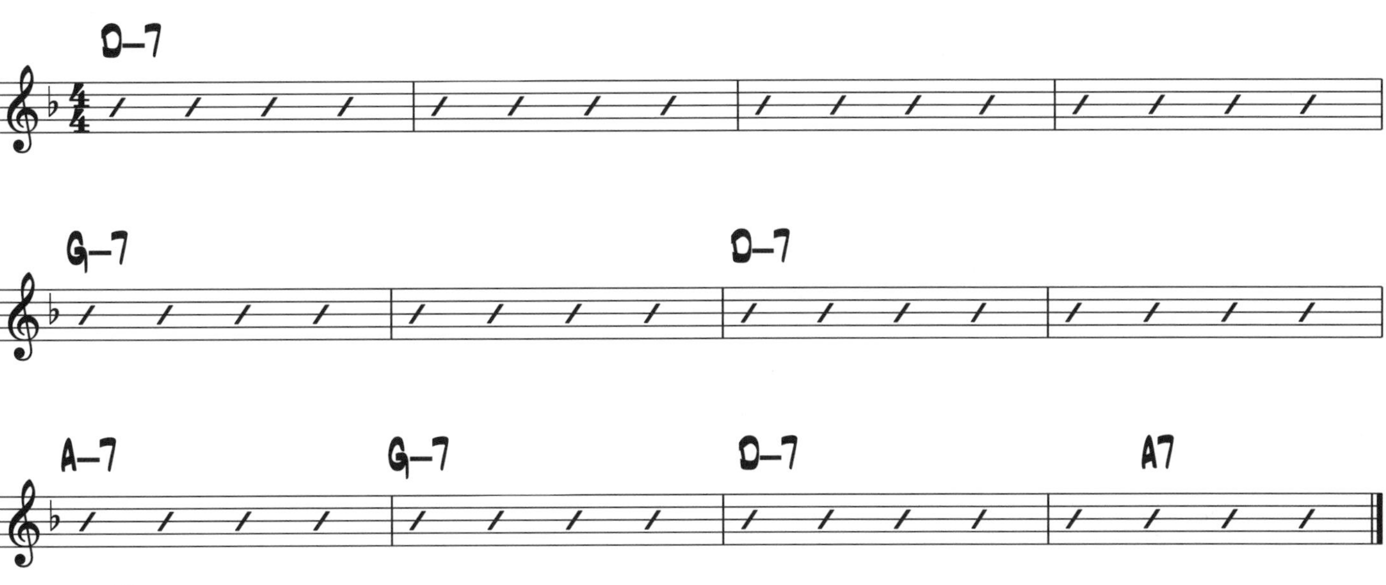

LISTEN 15 PLAY

Listen to "I Just Wanna Be With You." Is there an introduction or ending? What part of the form did these added sections come from?

This is the arrangement used on the recording:

Intro	Head: 2x	Sax Solo: 2x	Head	Ending
4 Measures	1 Chorus = 12 Measures	1 Chorus = 12 Measures	1 Chorus = 12 Measures	8 Measures

The intro and ending come from the form's last four measures. On the recording, the band chose to play the ending twice. This kind of repeated ending is called a *tag ending.*

PERFORMANCE TIP

Sometimes, a band may decide to "tag a tune" (play a tag ending) several times, building energy with each repetition. If things are going well and everyone is in the mood, a band may even make an ending longer than the rest of the tune. This is a place where people really let loose and have fun playing. When you listen to music, pay attention to what a band is doing at the end of a tune.

IDEAS FOR IMPROVISING: D BLUES SCALE

The D blues scale is a good one for this tune:

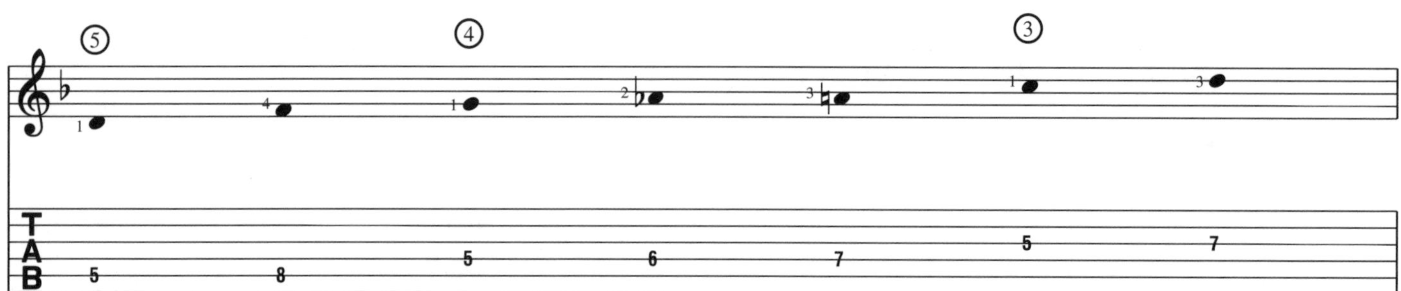

Here are all the notes of the D blues scale available in the fifth position:

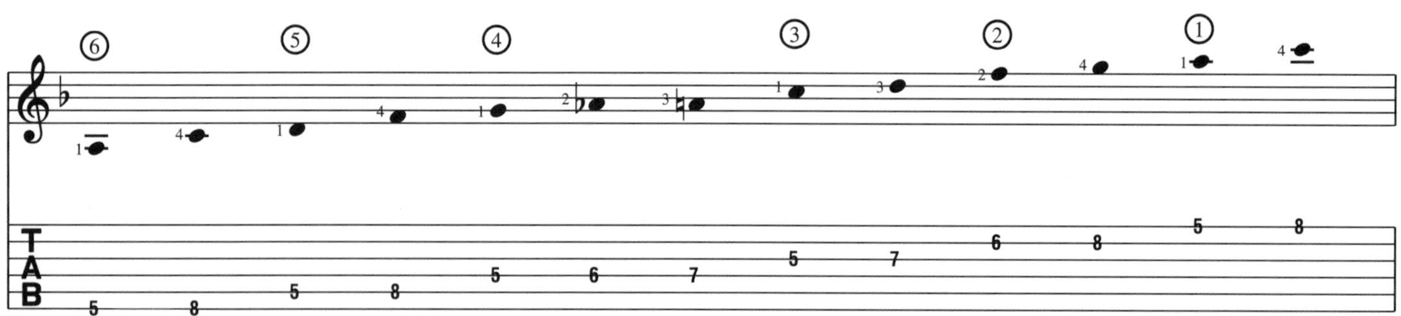

LISTEN 16 PLAY

Practice the D blues scale in the fifth position, up and down, with the recording. Play each note in steady time, one per beat, and play as evenly as you can. Some notes, especially blue notes such as the A♭, will jump out at you. Think about these notes when you create your own solo.

CALL AND RESPONSE

1. Echo each phrase, exactly as you hear it.
2. Improvise an answer to each phrase. Imitate the sound and rhythmic feel of the phrase you hear, and use the notes from the D blues scale.

LISTEN 17 PLAY

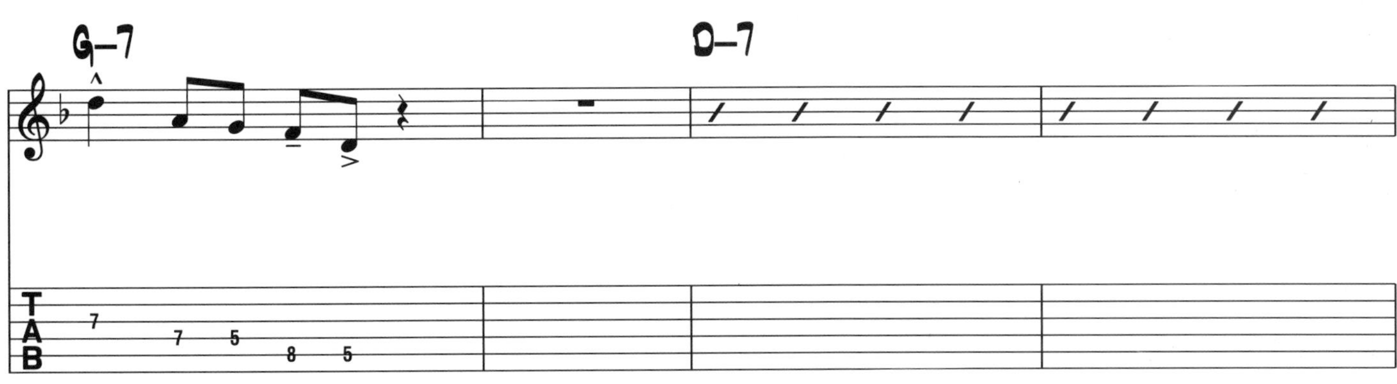

LISTEN 18 PLAY

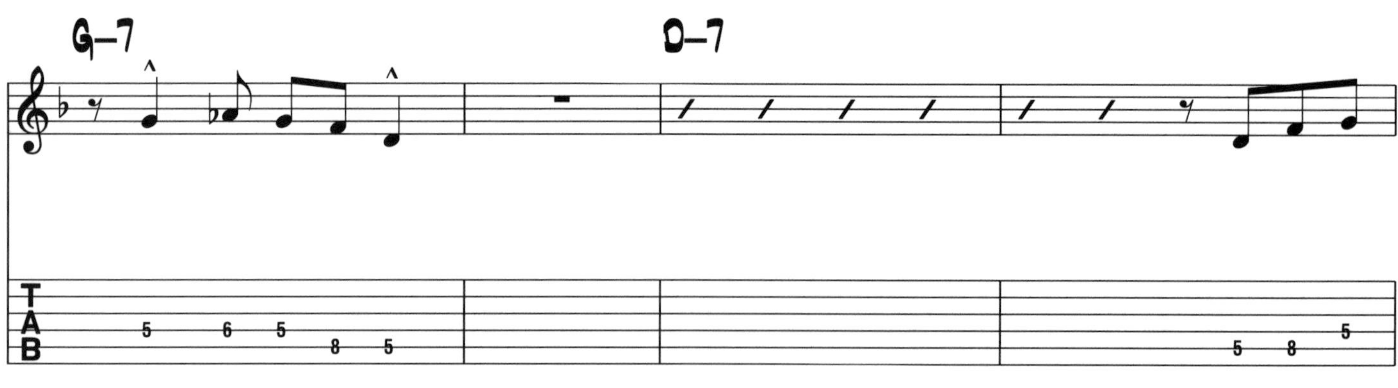

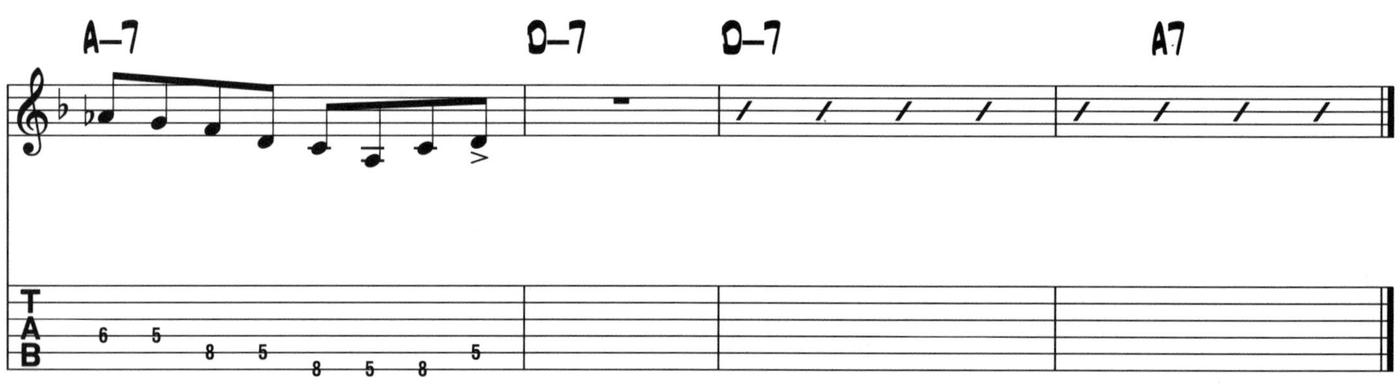

Write out a few of your own ideas. Use the D blues scale.

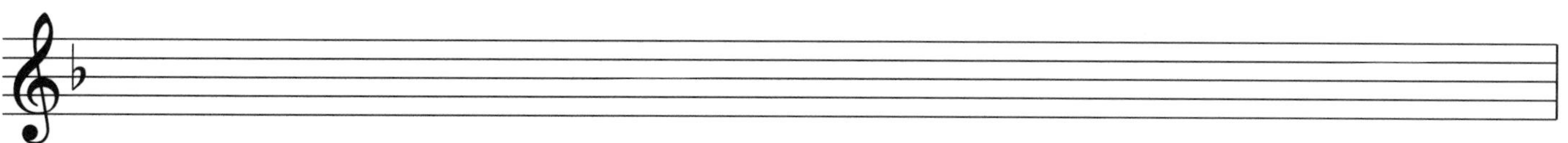

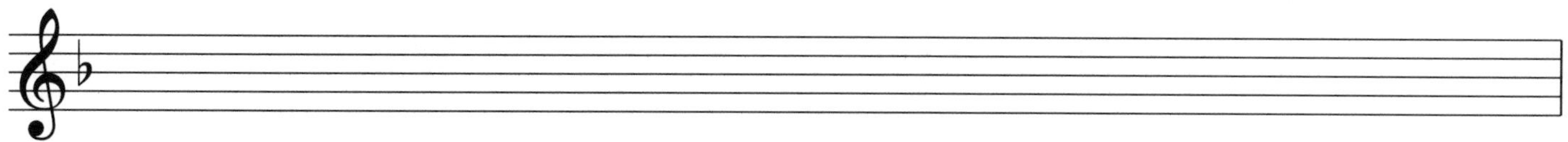

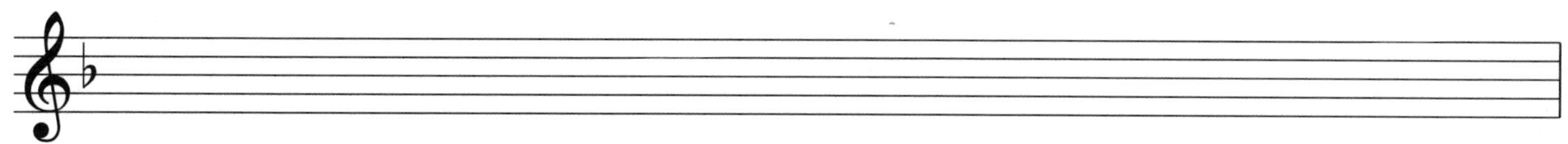

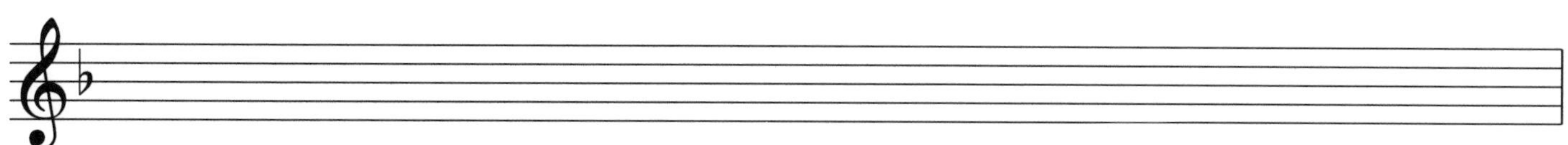

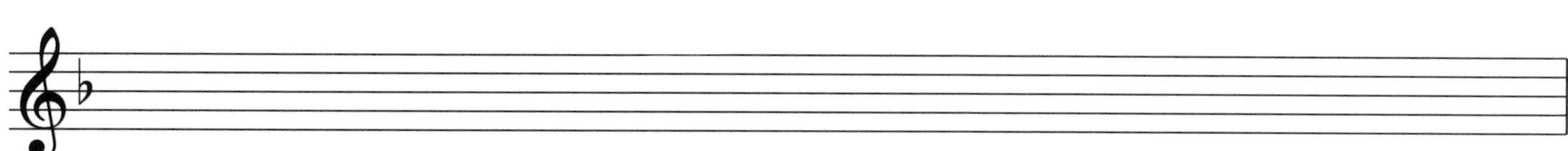

LISTEN 16 PLAY

Create a one-chorus solo using any techniques you have learned. Memorize your solo and practice it along with the recording.

LESSON 12
READING

GUITAR PART

Play "I Just Wanna Be With You" while reading from the written guitar part. Play it as written.

LISTEN 16 PLAY

I Just Wanna Be With You

Guitar Part

By Matt Marvuglio

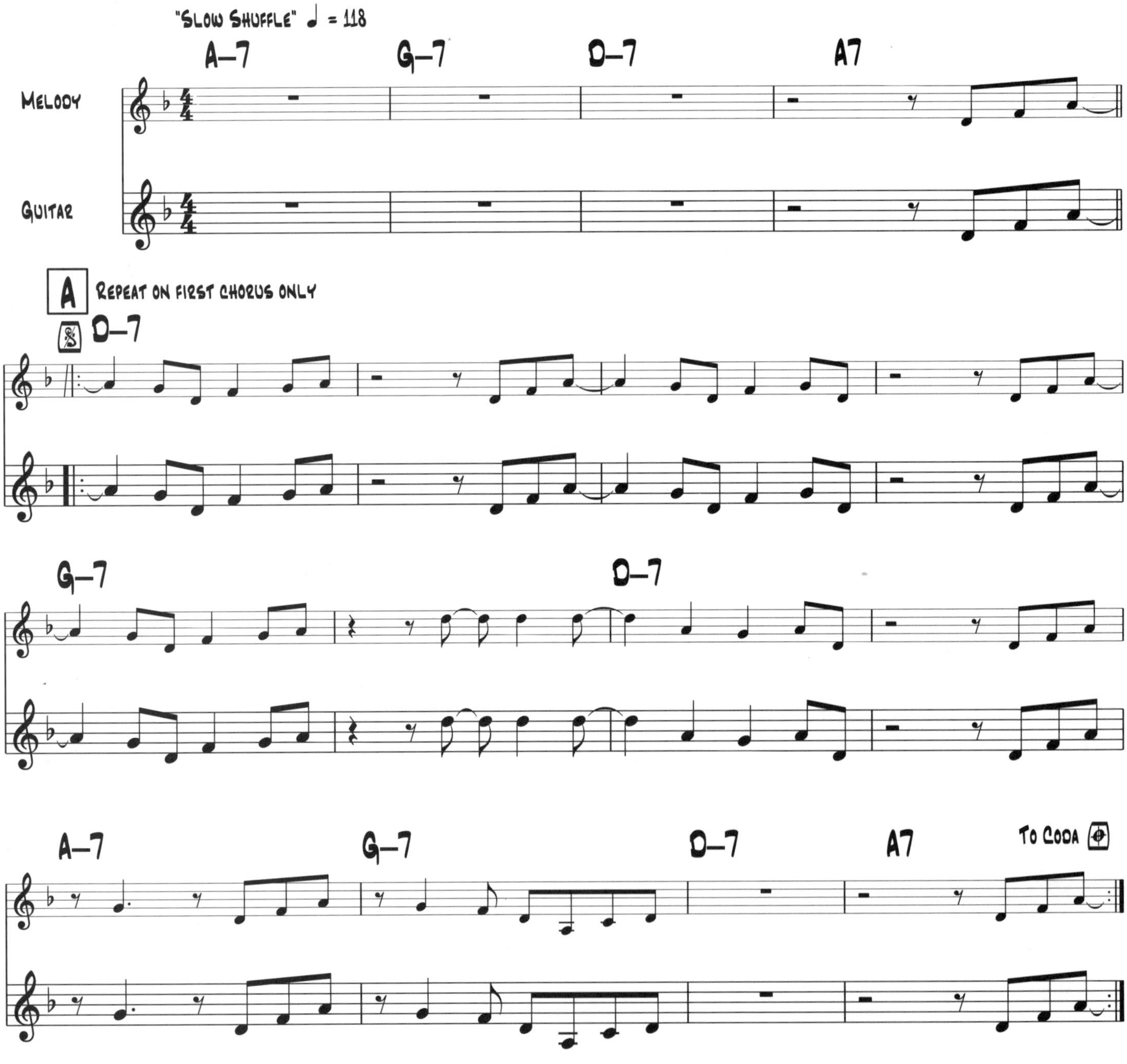

B
SOLOS
D–7
G–7
D–7
A–7
G–7
D–7
AFTER SOLOS, D.S. AL G
A7
2
CODA
A–7
G–7
D–7
A–7
G–7
D–7

LEAD SHEET

Play "I Just Wanna Be With You" from the lead sheet, using your own comping part. There are two new notation items here.

(𝄽 𝅗𝅥.) Break your regular comping rhythm when you see this (last measure) and play this rhythm instead.

INTRO/ENDING Though this lead sheet doesn't show an introduction or ending, you and your band can create your own. The intro can be just drums, as you saw in "Do It Now," or it can come from the last line of the tune, as it does in the recording of this tune. Tag the ending at least three times, repeating the last four measures of the written part.

LISTEN 16 PLAY

I JUST WANNA BE WITH YOU

BY MATT MARVUGLIO

CHAPTER III
DAILY PRACTICE ROUTINE

POSITION PLAYING

The guitar lets you play the same notes in more than one place. For example, on this tune, you might play that first note D on any of three strings:

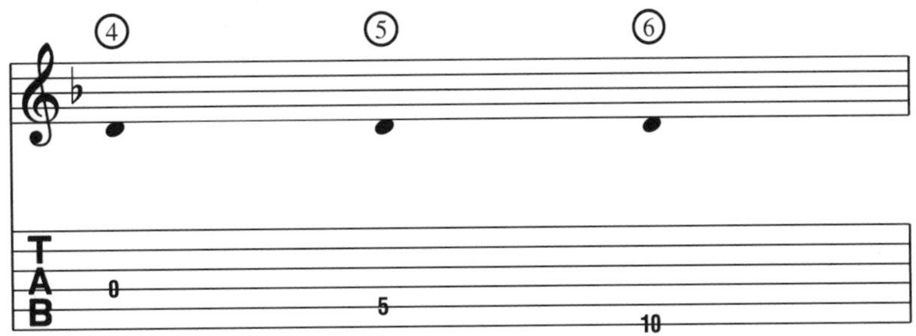

PRACTICE TIP

Choosing the right string will help minimize hand motion. It will also help you avoid open strings. Open strings can't be controlled as well as fingered strings. It is more difficult to stop them from ringing. They also have a different sound, and tend to stick out, when played against fingered notes. You can't do some special effects on open string notes, such as vibrato or bends. Of course, sometimes you'll want their unique sound, or you'll need them for chords, but generally, it's a good idea to find another way of playing open-string notes.

LISTEN 16 PLAY

Try the melody to "I Just Wanna Be With You" playing the D on the 5th string, using the following fingerings:

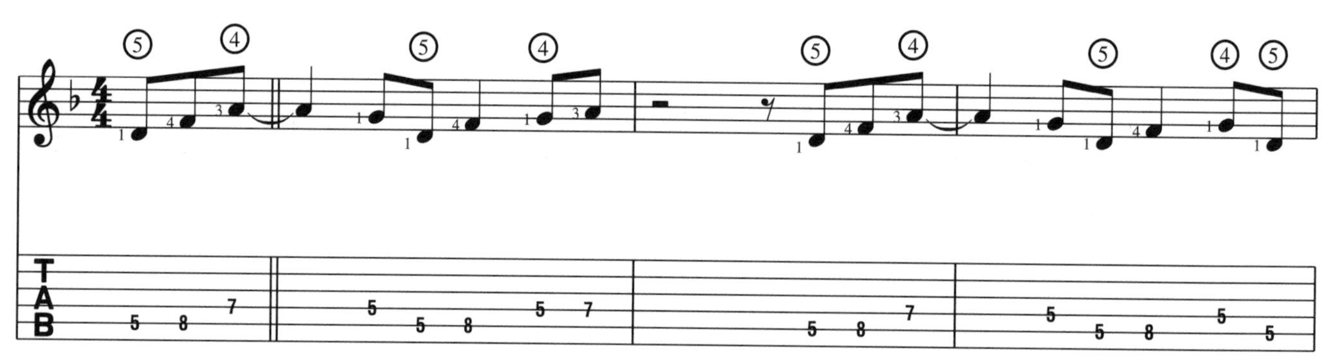

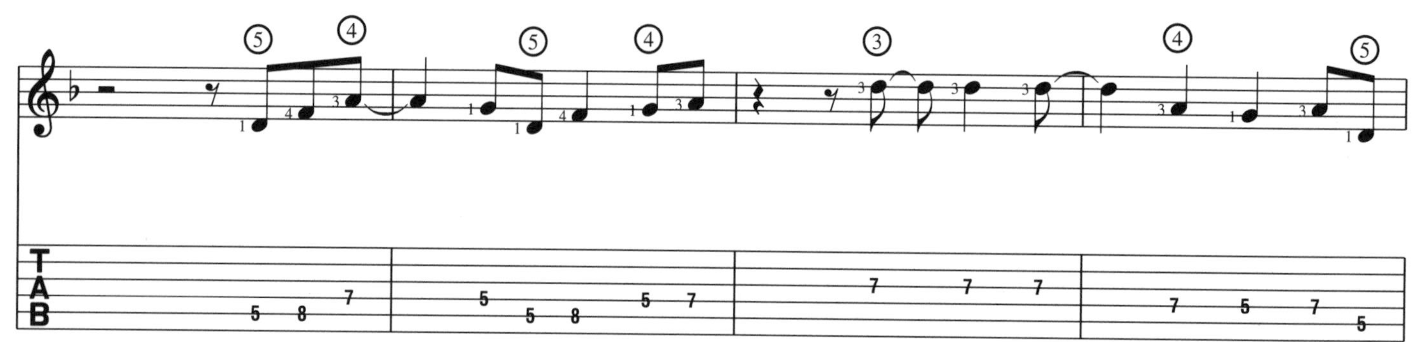

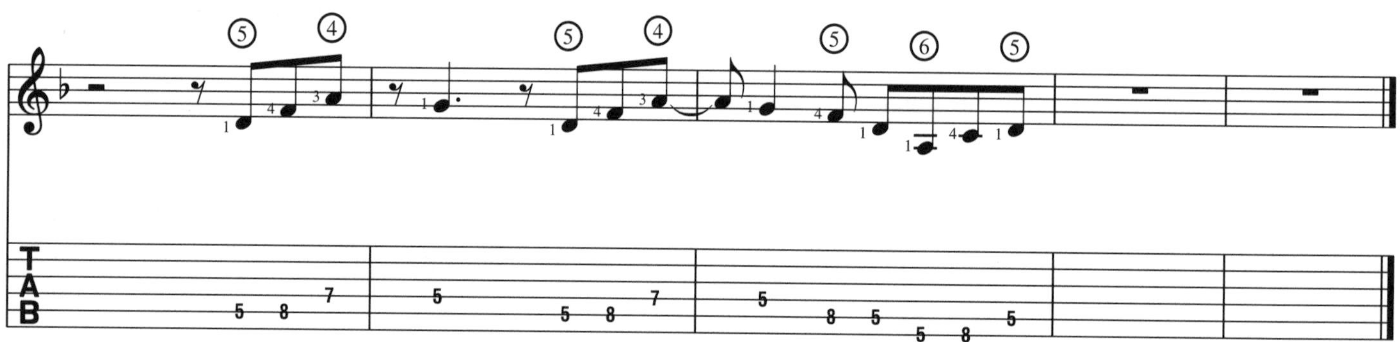

When your first finger is on the fifth fret like this, it is in *fifth position.* The position number is just the fret number where your first finger plays. So, tenth position would be when your first finger is on the tenth fret.

CHALLENGE

Try to play the melody to "I Just Wanna Be With You" in tenth position. Why is fifth position a better choice?

LEARNING THE GROOVE: ACCENTS

In "I Just Wanna Be With You," almost every beat has eighth notes. They are played as triplets, but some are *accented*—played louder—than others. Accented notes are marked with a ">" symbol.

LISTEN 15 PLAY

Listen to the three notes that begin each phrase of "I Just Wanna Be With You." What's different about the way that these three notes are played? Is one louder? More accented? Hit harder? Listen to this figure at the beginning of every phrase.

The accent mark shows that the third note is always stressed. This is common in swing music, and it gives the rhythm a syncopated, lively feel.

Again, with the recording, tap your foot with the pulse, sing the melody, and play dampened strings where you see an accent. Do this through the whole tune.

Now, play the melody, accenting the notes as marked. Notice that the accented notes are on weak beats. This gives the groove a swinging, syncopated feel. Make sure that eighth notes played before rests are held long enough, ending right at the next beat, not before.

LISTEN 16 PLAY

CALL AND RESPONSE: LICKS

1. Echo each lick, exactly as you hear it.
2. Improvise an answer to each lick. Imitate the sound and rhythmic feel of the lick you hear, and use the notes from the D blues scale. Try to imitate the articulations you hear on the recording.

LISTEN 19 PLAY

T
A
B
7 7 7 8 5 7
8 8
T
A
B
7 7 7 7 7
8 8 7 5
T
A
B
5 8 7
7 7 5 5
7 8 5
T
A
B
7 8 5 7
8 5 8 7
T
A
B
7 7 7 7 7 7
7 5 7 5

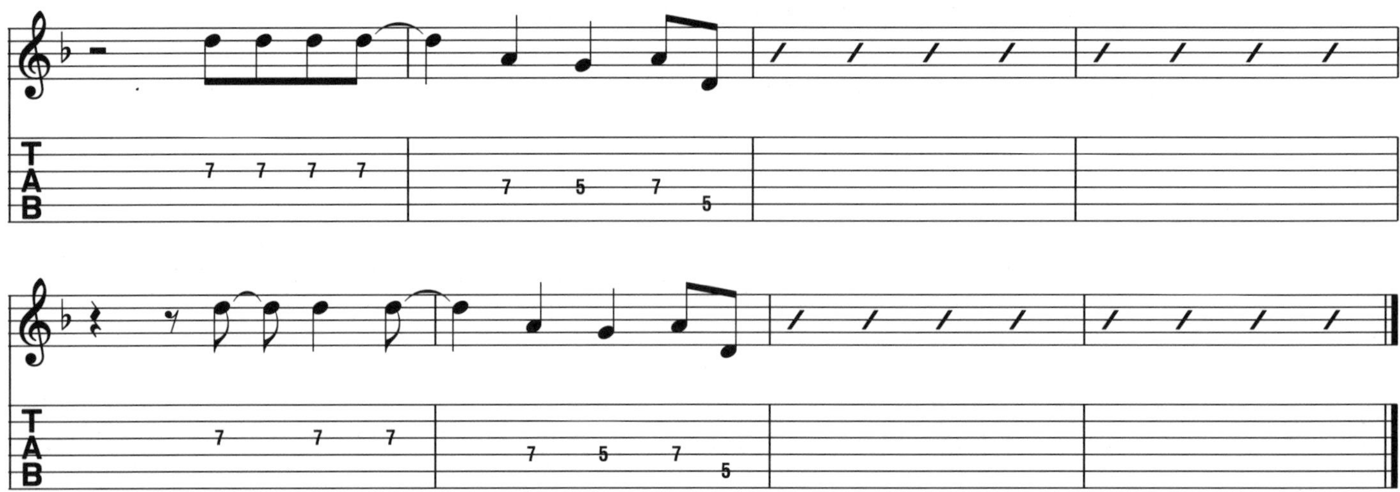

Write out a few of your own ideas. Use the D blues scale.

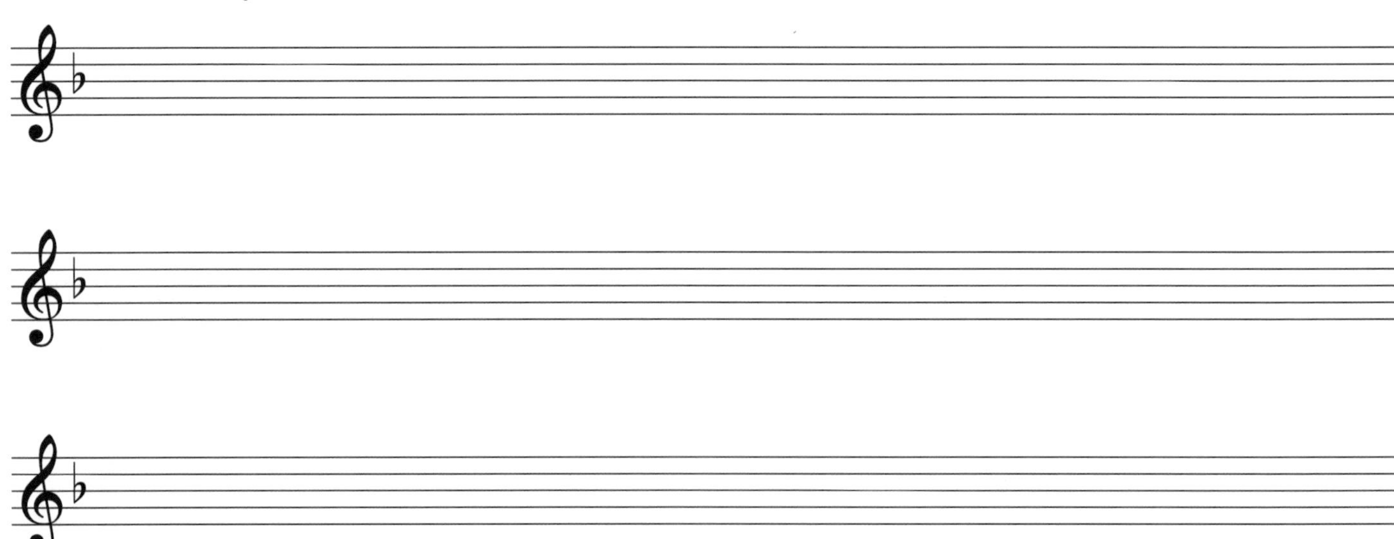

LISTEN 16 PLAY

Create a one-chorus solo using any techniques you have learned. Memorize your solo and practice it along with the recording.

PERFORMANCE TIP

Once you can play the melody to "I Just Wanna Be With You," practice it with different kinds of accents on the notes. Try it very softly, then very loudly, then softly again. Play the notes as short and as lightly as possible, so that they sound very individual and isolated. Then play them long, with one note flowing into the next. Keep the same written rhythmic values; just experiment with different ways of playing the melody. Finally, mix up all these options, playing some notes accented, some short, some long. Find a combination of articulations for the melody that feels natural. This will make your interpretation unique, and help you develop your own style.

IDEAS FOR IMPROVISING: CHORD TONES

So far, we've been building our improvised solos from scales. In "I Just Wanna Be With You," we've been using the D blues scale:

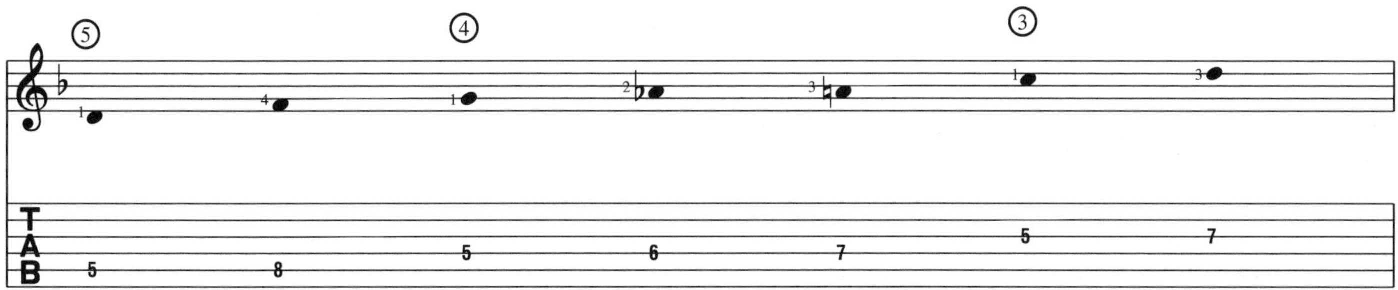

Another source of good notes is the chords played by the rest of the band. The lead sheet shows three chords: D–7, G–7, and A–7. Here they are:

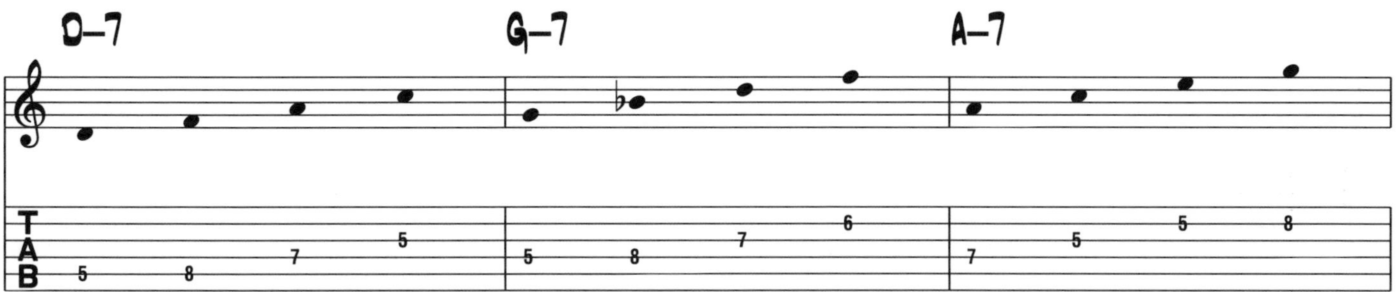

Chord tones always sound natural in a melody. Here's a chord-tone melody based on the D–7 chord. Though the notes are also all from the D blues scale, this kind of chord-tone melody has its own feel:

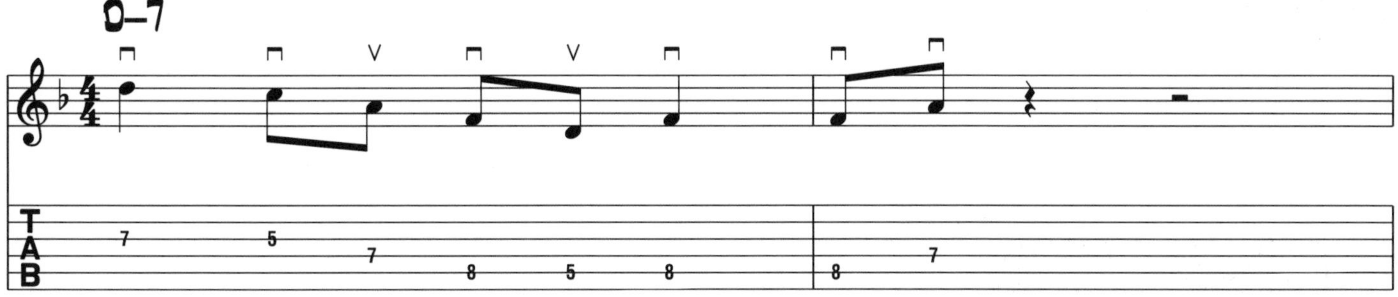

The other chord in this tune is A–7. Which new notes can we find in this chord to add to the D–7 chord tones?

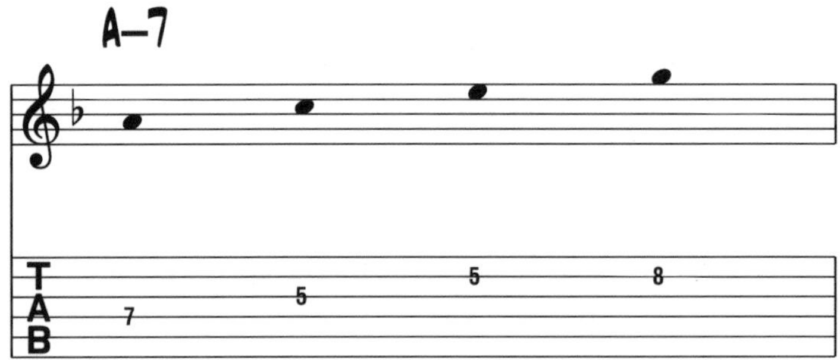

By combining notes from the tune's chords, we can create phrases such as this one, which would work well as the third phrase:

When you improvise, look at the lead sheet, and see what chord tones are used in the tune. They will be a good resource for your solo.

SOLO PRACTICE

Practice the following melody and play it along with the recording. It is based on the blues scale and the chords found in "I Just Wanna Be With You." Then create your own solo using the same chords and scales.

LISTEN 16 PLAY

MEMORIZE

LISTEN 16 PLAY

Create your own comping part and improvised solo to "I Just Wanna Be With You." Practice it along with the recording, and memorize it.

PLAY "I JUST WANNA BE WITH YOU" WITH YOUR OWN BAND!

PLAYING FUNK

CHAPTER IV

"Leave Me Alone" is a *funk* tune. Funk has its roots in New Orleans street music. It started in the 1960s and is a combination of rock, r&b, Motown, jazz, and blues. Funk has also influenced many rap artists. To hear more funk, listen to artists such as James Brown, Tower of Power, Kool and the Gang, the Meters, the Yellowjackets, Chaka Khan, Tina Turner, and the Red Hot Chili Peppers.

LESSON 13
TECHNIQUE/THEORY

Listen to "Leave Me Alone," and play along with the recording. Try to match the guitar. This is another blues tune, in which you play the melody at the head and comp chords during the solos. The form is the same as the other blues tunes you have played, but the funk groove is new.

LISTEN 20 PLAY

This is the melody:

This is the comping part:

First Pattern **Second Pattern** **Third Pattern**

CHORD PATTERNS

Listen to the guitar and keyboard comping patterns under the sax solo. The chords change quickly. The first pattern has these two chords. Note that there is no root in the G7 chord. The bass guitar and keyboard will play that note.

First Pattern:

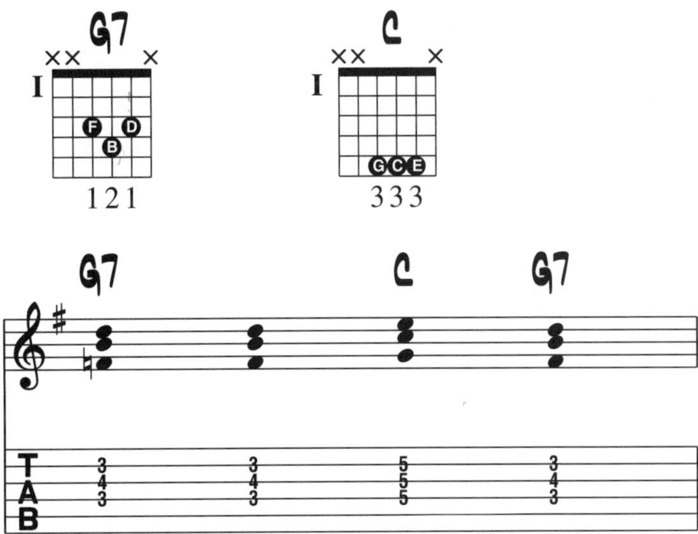

The secret of changing chords quickly is in choosing chord forms that are close to each other on the fretboard. For this pattern, if you use the chord forms above, you only need to move one finger (your third finger) to change from one chord to the next.

The second pattern is very similar. Again, by choosing the right chord forms in the right positions, you can switch chords by moving only your third finger. Since the chord forms shown in the first pattern are movable (they have no open strings), your fingers can stay in the same position for the second pattern. The only difference is that you start on a different fret.

Second Pattern:

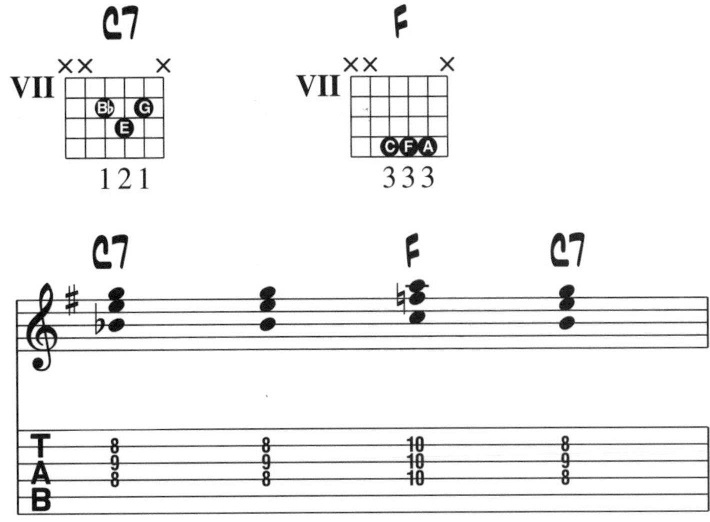

In the third pattern, your hand position remains the same. It moves from the eighth fret to the tenth fret.

Third Pattern:

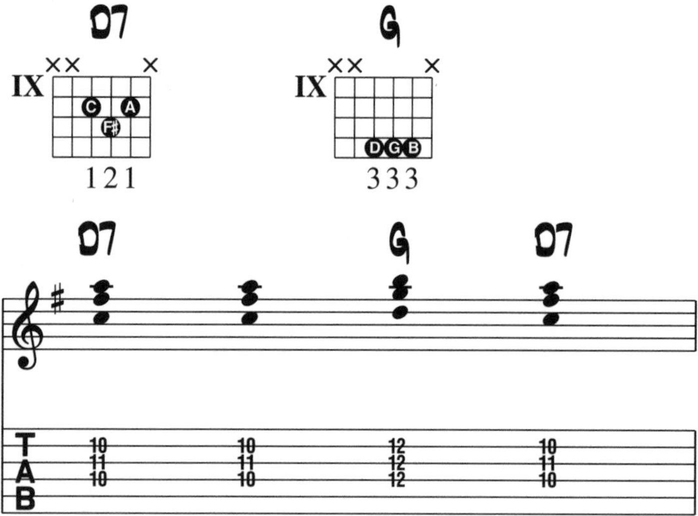

LISTEN 20 PLAY

Practice these three comping patterns and then play them along with the recording.

COMPING AT THE HEAD

At the head, the comping part (just keyboard, on the recording) is simpler than the one during the solos. This works well because it makes the groove at the head sound slightly different than the groove during the solos. When you play this tune with your own band, you might choose to play rhythm guitar at the head, instead of melody, so you should learn both comping parts.

Practice "Leave Me Alone" playing a rhythm guitar part all the way through. At the head, play the comping part shown below. During the solos, play the comping part you learned earlier. Then switch back to this one when the head returns.

LISTEN 20 PLAY

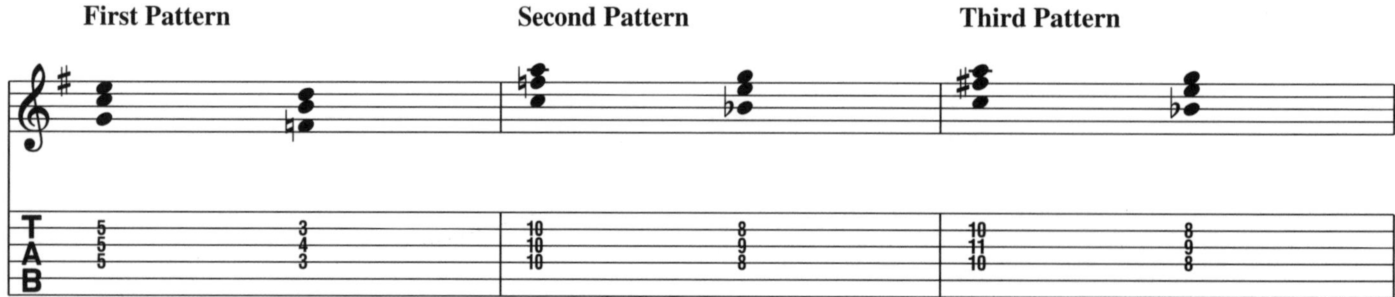

LESSON 14
LEARNING THE GROOVE

HOOKING UP TO FUNK

LISTEN 20 PLAY

Listen to "Leave Me Alone." This funk groove has its roots in New Orleans street music—funky march music played on marching instruments (snare drums, bass drums, and so on) still found in the Mardi Gras parades each spring. Many New Orleans artists were important to the development of funk.

Funk rhythms are played with less of a swing feel than blues. There is an underlying sixteenth-note feel, similar to rock. Beats 2 and 4 are often accented, usually by the snare drum.

Find the beat, and play dampened strings along with the strong, funk backbeat.

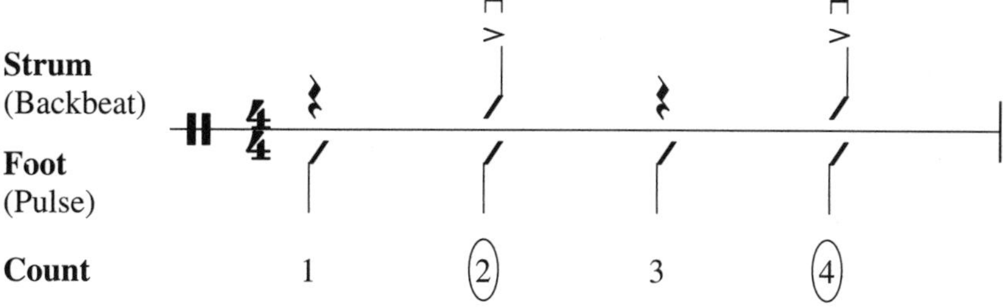

Funk has a sixteenth-note feel, like rock. Count sixteenths on each beat, as you strum along on the backbeat. The backbeat is particularly strong in funk.

Tap the quarter-note pulse with your foot, strum the backbeat, and count the sixteenths. When you are ready, do this along with the recording.

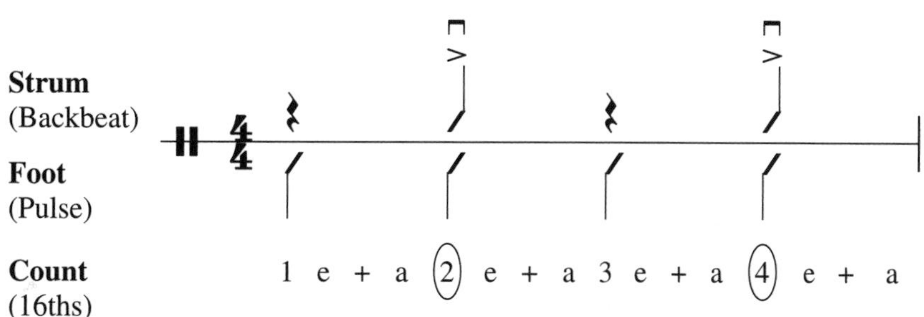

SYNCOPATION

In the last chapter, you learned to play syncopated swing eighth notes. In funk, syncopations are often on sixteenth notes. The rhythm guitar part to "Leave Me Alone" has a syncopated sixteenth note at the end of the first beat. This note interrupts the regular pulse. Like the strong backbeat and the sixteenth-note feel, syncopation is common in funk.

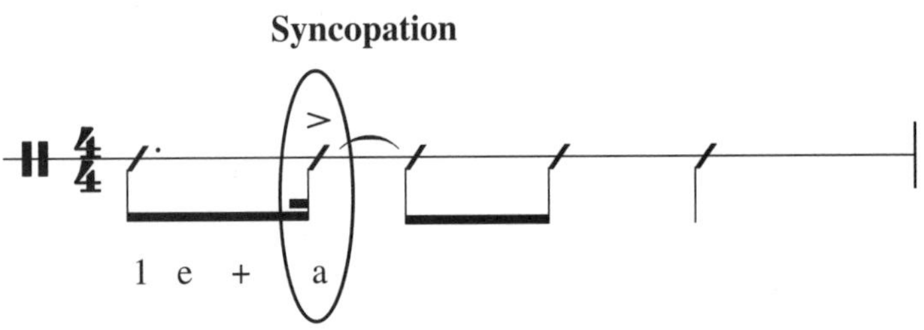

LEARNING "LEAVE ME ALONE"

LISTEN 20 PLAY

Play the rhythms of the rhythm-guitar part (played during the solos). Accent the syncopation. When you are ready, play along with the recording.

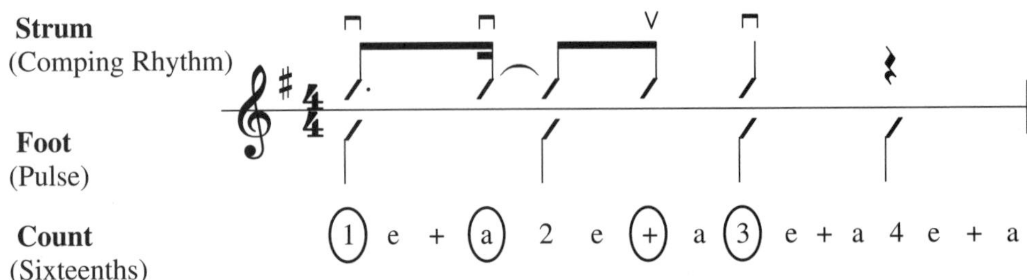

LISTEN 20 PLAY

Play your comping part using the written rhythms. While you play, count the sixteenths, and hook up with the groove.

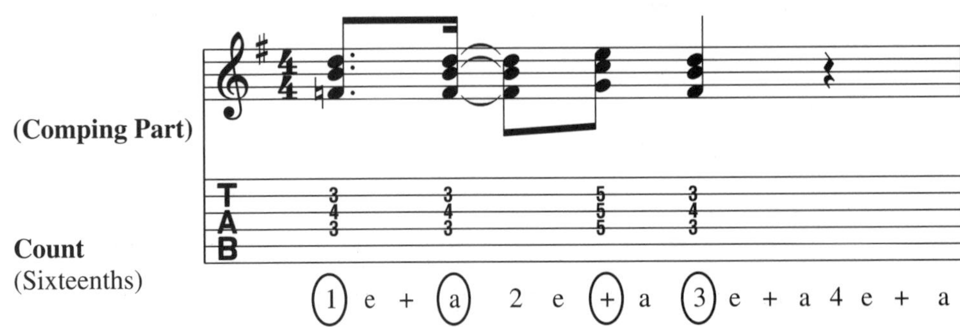

LESSON 15
IMPROVISATION

FORM AND ARRANGEMENT

Listen to "Leave Me Alone" and follow the form. This funk tune follows the 12-bar blues form.

LISTEN 20 PLAY

On the recording, the arrangement begins with a four-measure introduction, featuring the rhythm section playing the groove.

INTRO	HEAD: 2X	SOLO: 2X	HEAD
4 Measures	1 Chorus = 12 Measures	1 Chorus = 12 Measures	1 Chorus = 12 Measures

IDEAS FOR IMPROVISING:

SCALE

The G blues scale is a good one for this tune.

MELODIC SEQUENCE

Another technique for improvisation is *melodic sequencing*—taking a lick, and repeating it several times, beginning on different pitches. This lick comes from the G blues scale.

Play this lick in third position.

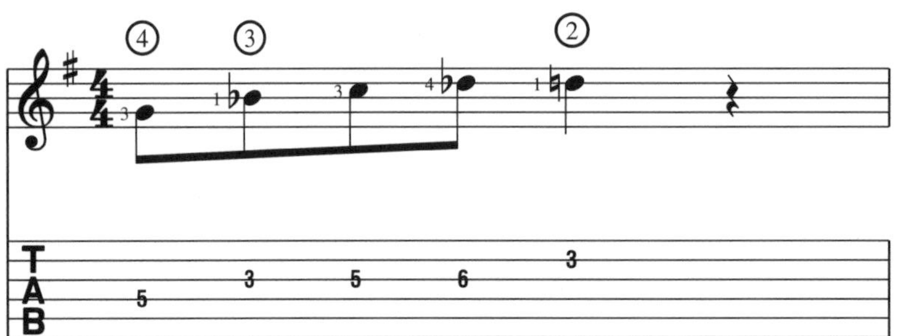

Move this lick to eighth position, on the same strings, starting on C. Notice that the fingering is the same.

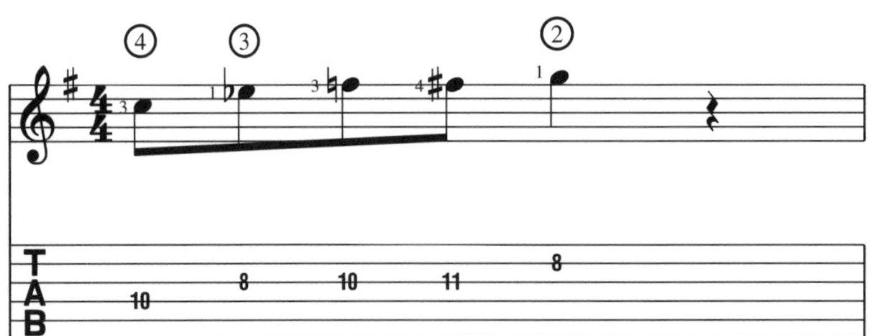

Now, play it in tenth position, on the same strings, starting on D. Again, the fingering is the same.

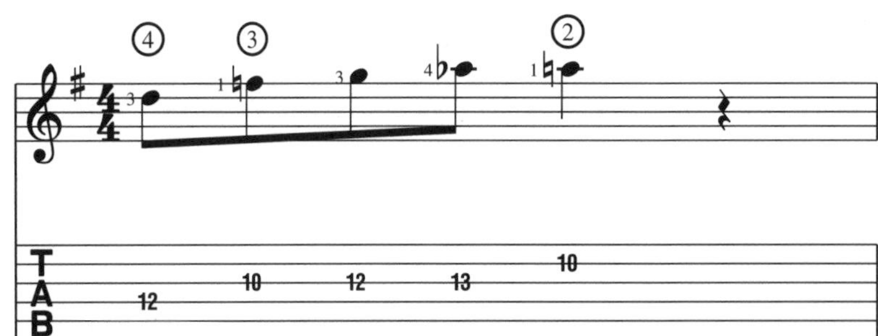

MELODIC SEQUENCE PRACTICE

You can create an entire solo using this technique. In the following melody, the same lick is reused, starting on different notes.

Practice this solo with the recording.

CALL AND RESPONSE

1. Echo each phrase exactly as you hear it.
2. Improvise an answer to each phrase. Imitate the sound and rhythmic feel of the phrase you hear, and use the notes from the G blues scale.

LISTEN 22 PLAY

Listen **Play**

G7

C7 G7

D7 C7 G7

LISTEN 23 PLAY

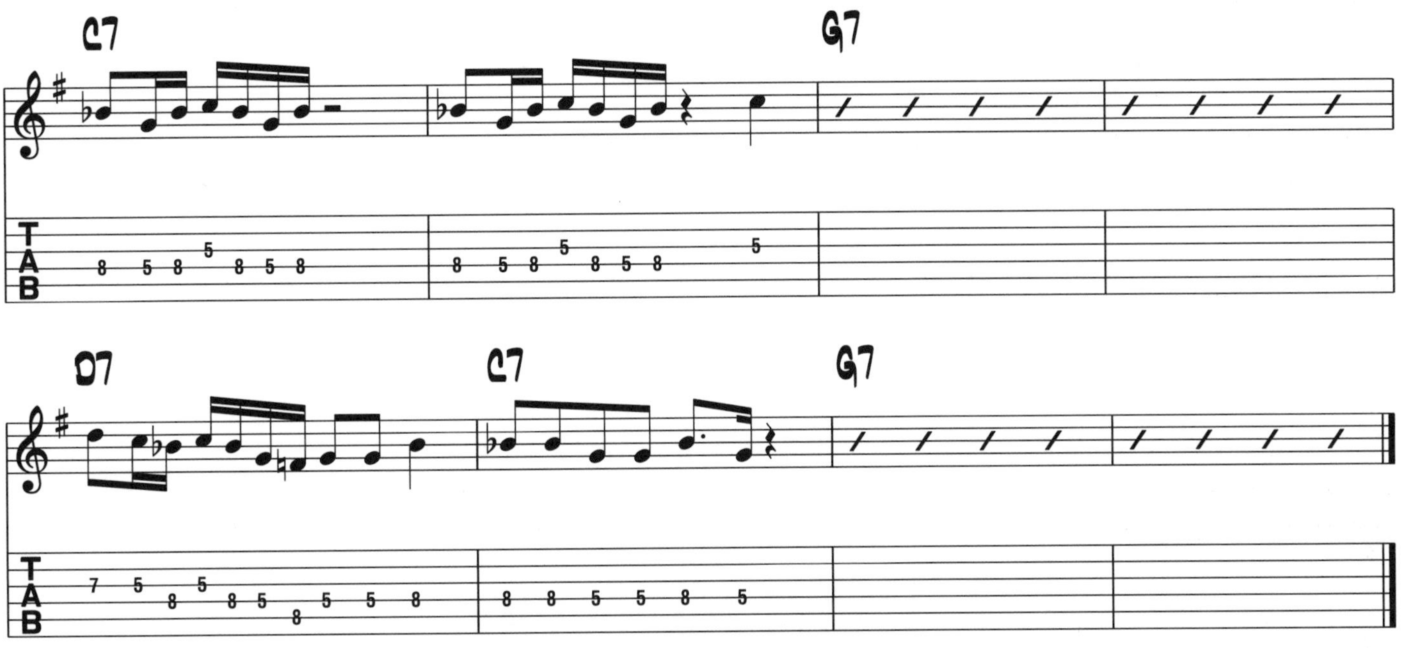

Write out a few of your own ideas.

LISTEN 21 PLAY

Create a one-chorus solo using any techniques you have learned. Memorize your solo and practice it along with the recording.

LESSON 16
READING

GUITAR PART

4 A bar with a number over it means that you should rest for that number of measures. The introduction here is just bass and drums, so you can sit out. But count along, so you are ready to come in on the fifth measure.

Play "Leave Me Alone" along with the recording, using the written guitar part.

LEAVE ME ALONE

GUITAR PART

BY MATT MARVUGLIO

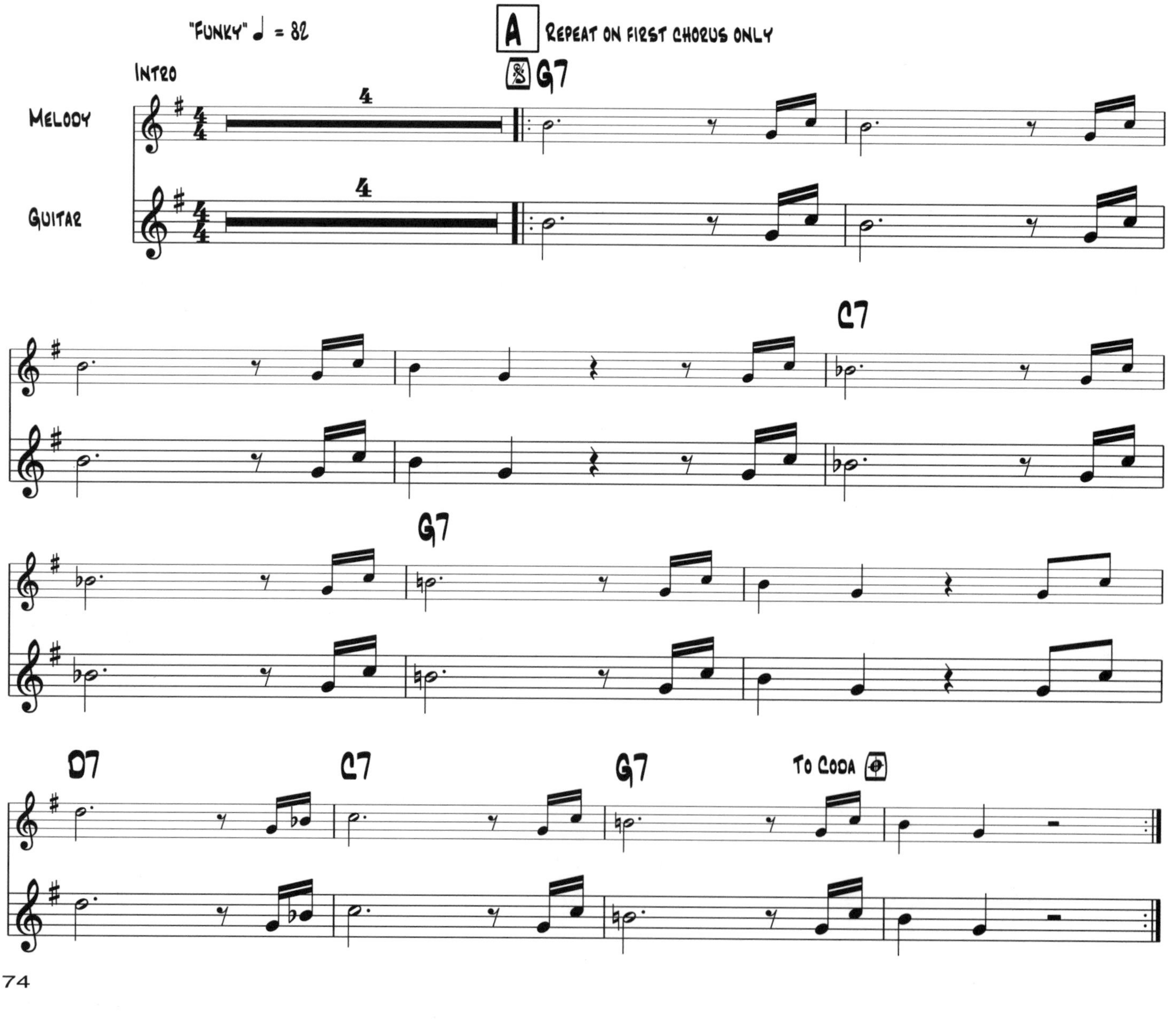

"FUNKY" ♩ = 82

A REPEAT ON FIRST CHORUS ONLY

INTRO

MELODY

GUITAR

4

G7

C7

G7

D7 C7 G7 TO CODA

B
SOLOS
G7
C7
G7
D7
C7
G7
AFTER SOLOS, D.S. AL
CODA

LEAD SHEET

Play "Leave Me Alone" and follow along with the lead sheet. Create your own solo using a melodic sequence.

LISTEN 21 PLAY

Leave Me Alone

By Matt Marvuglio

PRACTICE TIP

Memorizing your notes makes it easier to follow arrangement directions, such as "D.S. al ⊕."

CHAPTER IV
DAILY PRACTICE ROUTINE

PICKING SIXTEENTHS

The right picking choice helps you play faster. Try this picking pattern on open strings:

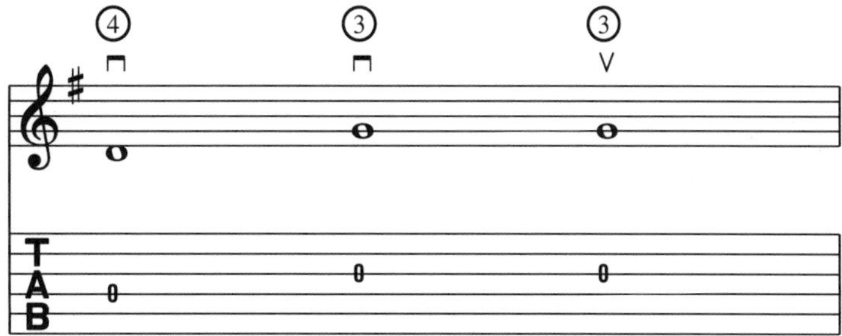

This is a good picking choice for the sixteenth-note figures ending each lick in "Leave Me Alone." Try it on the first lick:

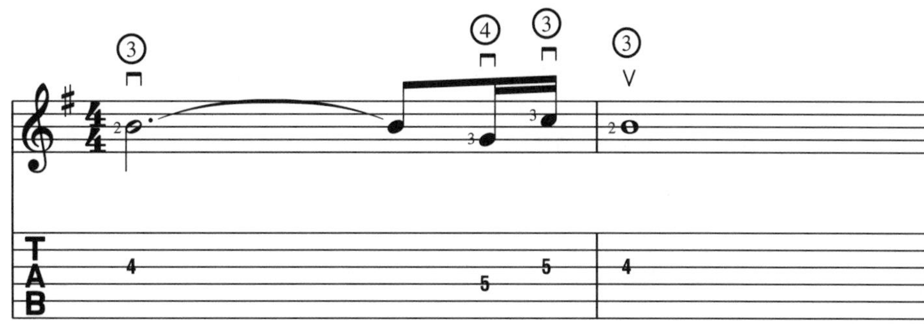

This down-down-up motion lets you play the lick without wasting any motion. Try it once using all down-strokes. The picking shown above is much easier. Practice it all the way up the fretboard.

COMPING PRACTICE

Play this comping part along with the recording, using the chord forms you learned in the lessons.

LISTEN 21 PLAY

Now, play this comping part.

As you can see, there is more than one way to comp on this tune. On the recording, the first one above was played at the head and the second one at the solo.

LISTEN 21 PLAY

Create your own comping part to "Leave Me Alone," using your own rhythms or chords. Practice it with the recording. Make it funky!

IMPROVISATION AND MELODY

LISTEN 21 PLAY

Another good source of improvising ideas is the melody itself. In this example, the written melody to "Leave Me Alone" is simplified, using just the main notes. Try it out with the recording.

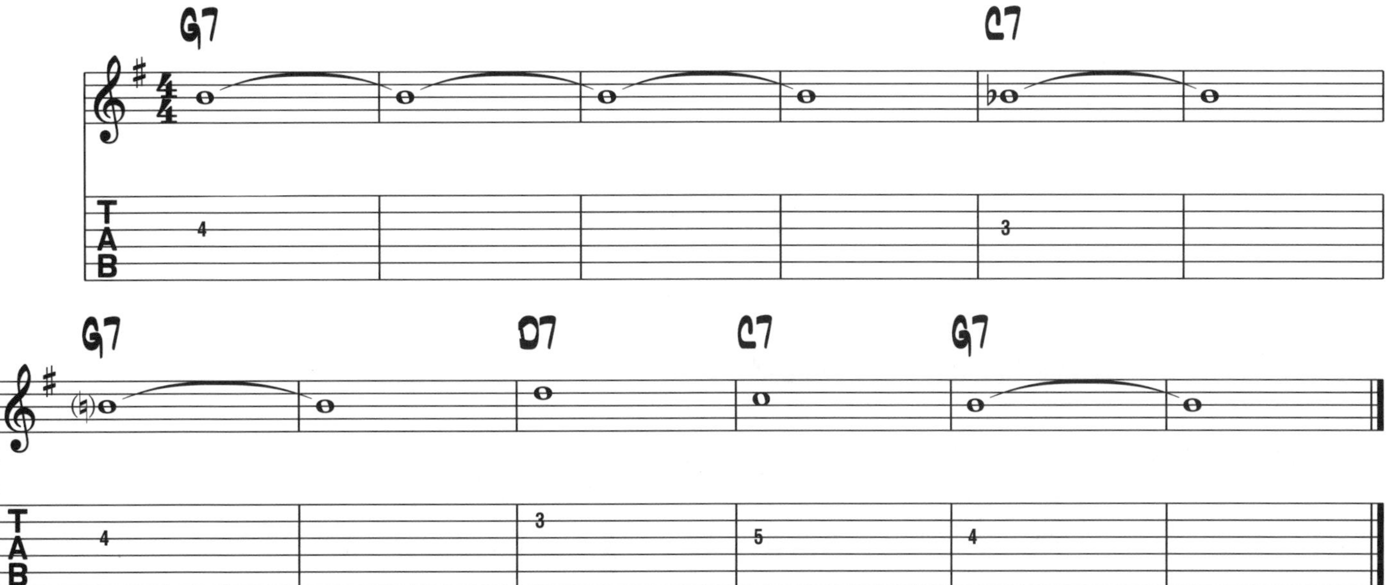

These notes form the melody's backbone, and can be used as the basis for your own solo too. Practice this solo with the recording, and notice how it uses the main notes of the melody (along with notes from the pentatonic scale). Then write your own solo using this technique.

MEMORIZE

LISTEN 21 PLAY

Create your own comping part and improvised solo to "Leave Me Alone." Practice it along with the recording, and memorize it.

SUMMARY

PLAY "LEAVE ME ALONE" WITH YOUR OWN BAND!

PLAYING LIGHT FUNK

CHAPTER V

"Affordable" is another funk tune, but it is lighter, with more of a feeling of open space. This style is popular with smooth-jazz artists. To hear more light funk, listen to artists such as David Sanborn, Earl Klugh, Walter Beasley, the Rippingtons, Dave Grusin, Kenny G, Bob James, and Anita Baker.

LESSON 17
TECHNIQUE/THEORY

Listen to "Affordable," and then play along with the recording. Try to match the guitar. This tune has two parts.

LISTEN 24 PLAY

In the first part, the guitar plays this comping pattern:

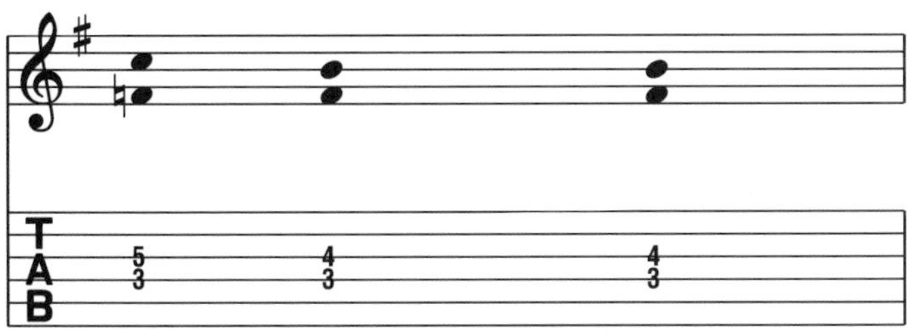

In the second part, the guitar plays this comping pattern:

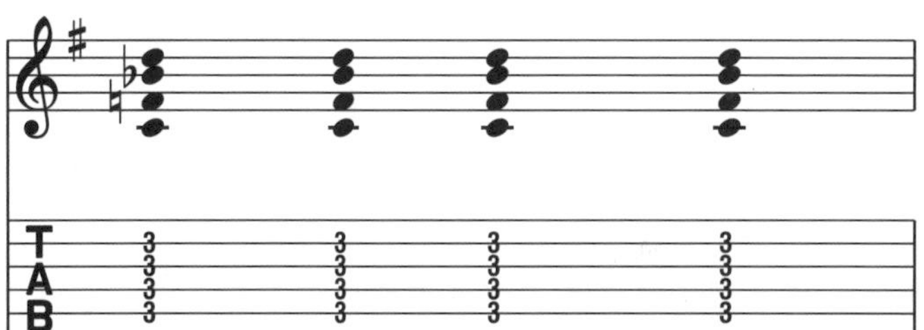

Play along with the recording and try to match these chords with the comping rhythms played by the guitar (and keyboard).

CHORDS

The first comping part in "Affordable" is very sparse, playing only two notes at once:

LISTEN 25 PLAY

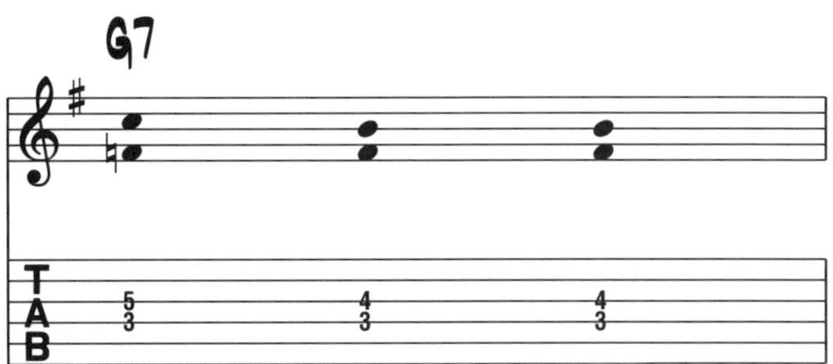

PRACTICE TIP

When you play this first pattern, keep holding down the B with your second finger, even when you play the C. You can then switch chords by moving just your third finger.

Even though the guitar plays only two notes, it is enough to create the whole character of the chord. That's because the notes chosen are the ones that are most important to the chord's sound: the 3 and the 7.

When comping, the root and fifth in a chord are often good notes to leave out. In this tune, the bass plays the root and the melody plays the fifth, so those notes are already in the air. You don't necessarily need to repeat them, especially when you are going for a clear, open sound.

The C, a fourth above the root (G), is a good tension note. Tension notes like this are called *suspensions*, and they are sometimes included in chord symbols (such as G7sus4)—especially when they are very prominent, or held for a long time. In this tune, since the suspended C quickly resolves to the B (a chord tone), the suspension is not included in the chord symbol.

The second chord pattern in this tune is much more dense and active.

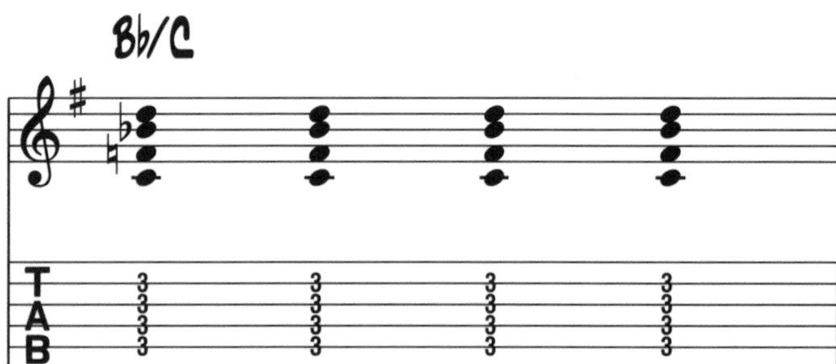

The symbol for this chord has two parts: B♭/C. This means that there is a B♭ chord played over the note C in the bass.

PRACTICE TIP

Strum down, not out. At the end of each stroke, the pick should rest on the first string.

LISTEN 26 PLAY

Practice the above patterns with the recording. Hook up with the guitar and keyboards, and play exactly the same rhythms.

LESSON 18
LEARNING THE GROOVE

HOOKING UP TO LIGHT FUNK

LISTEN 24 PLAY

Listen to "Affordable." This groove is built around eighth notes, with some syncopated sixteenths in the B section. Notice that the band hooks up with the bass drum.

To learn this feel, practice counting sixteenths, leaving out the middle two sixteenths of each beat. Count out loud, along with a metronome or click track on the quarter-note pulse.

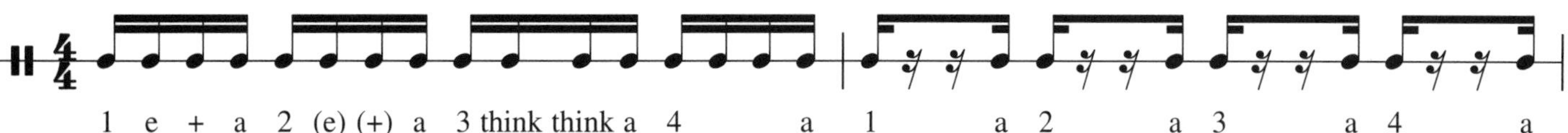

"Affordable" is a *light* funk tune. The guitar holds back more than it would with a *heavy* funk tune, such as "Leave Me Alone." To make it lighter, the whole rhythm section is quieter, and plays fewer notes. Like all funk, eighth notes are played straight, not swung. What were some of the other elements of funk you learned in the last chapter?

LISTEN 24 PLAY

Listen to "Affordable." Find the pulse, and play on the backbeat. The backbeat is still emphasized, but it is lighter than heavy funk.

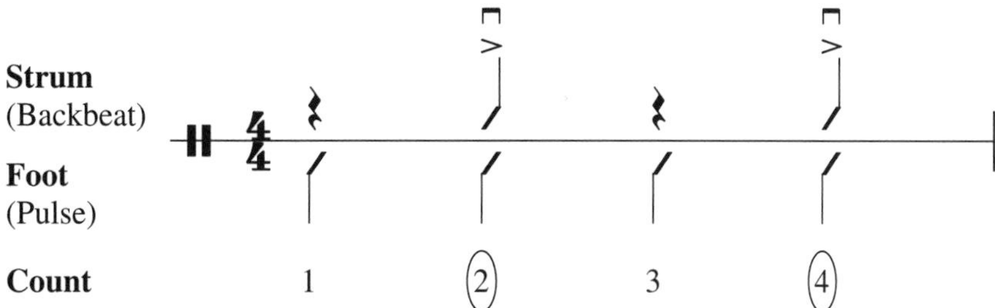

Tap the quarter-note pulse with your foot, play the backbeat, and count the sixteenths. When you are ready, do this along with the recording.

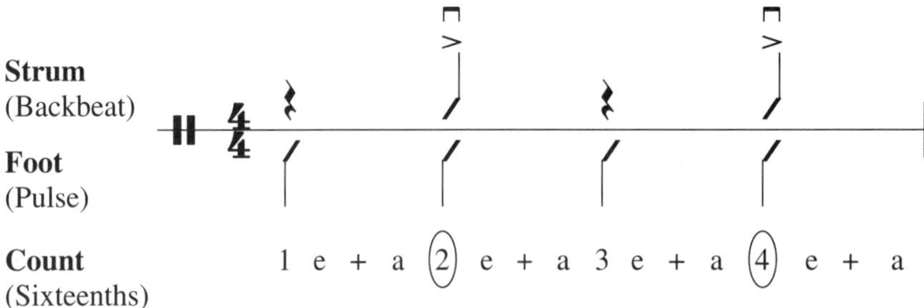

LEARNING "AFFORDABLE"

"Affordable" has two different parts with two different rhythmic feels. This first part has a lot of space. All instruments play very sparsely.

LISTEN 25 PLAY

Play the comping rhythms along with "Affordable." Accent the syncopations, but keep them light. When you are ready, tap along with the recording.

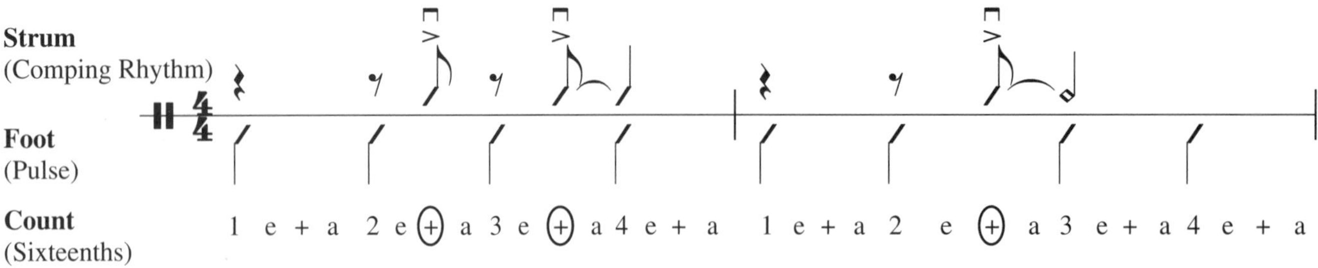

Play the comping part to "Affordable" along with the recording. Count the sixteenths, and try to match the rhythmic feel of the keyboard and guitar on the recording. Accent the syncopations.

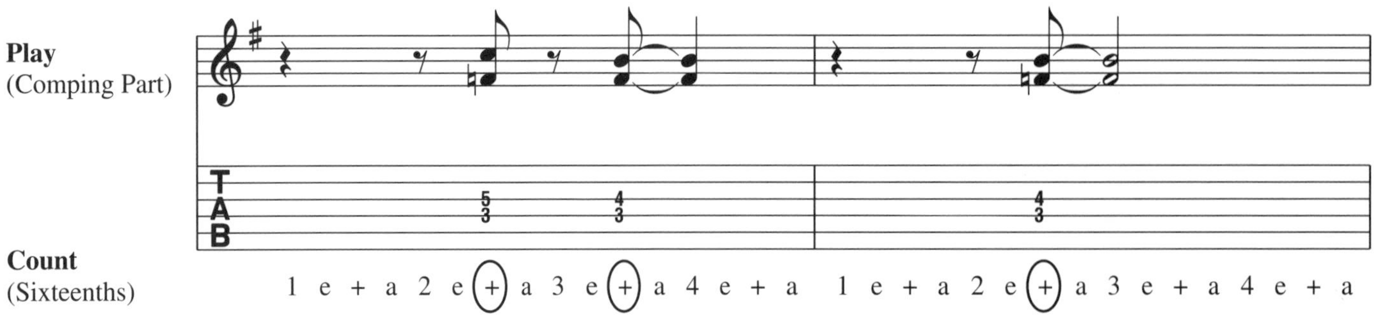

Play the comping rhythms to the second part of "Affordable." The second part has a stronger funk feel. It helps to establish a solid groove that supports the more active melody. When you are ready, play along with the recording.

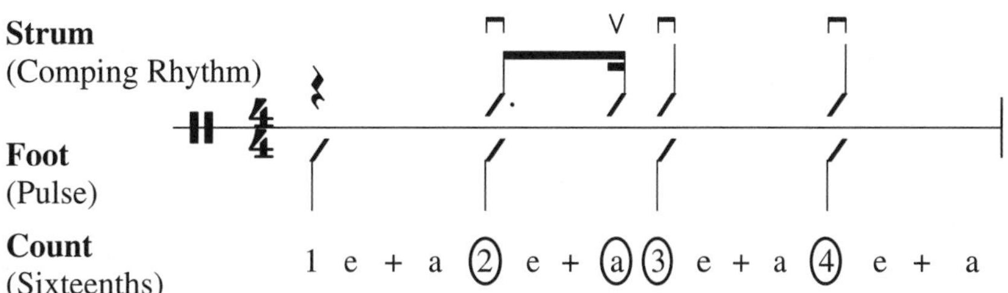

LISTEN 26 PLAY

Play the second written comping part. While you play, count the sixteenths, and hook up with the groove.

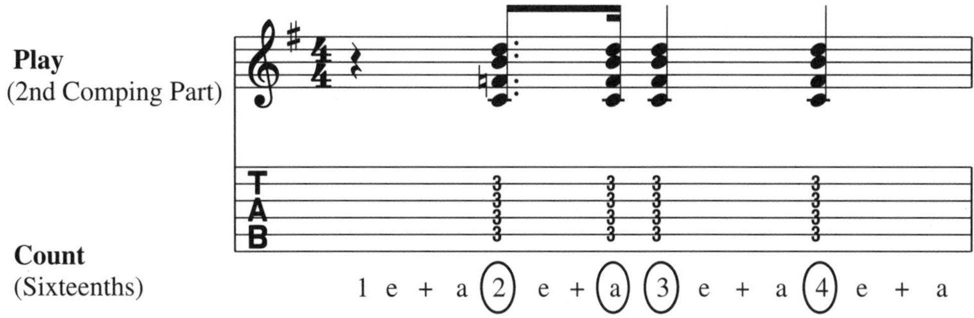

LESSON 19
IMPROVISATION

FORM AND ARRANGEMENT

Listen to "Affordable" and follow the 16-bar form.

LISTEN 24 PLAY

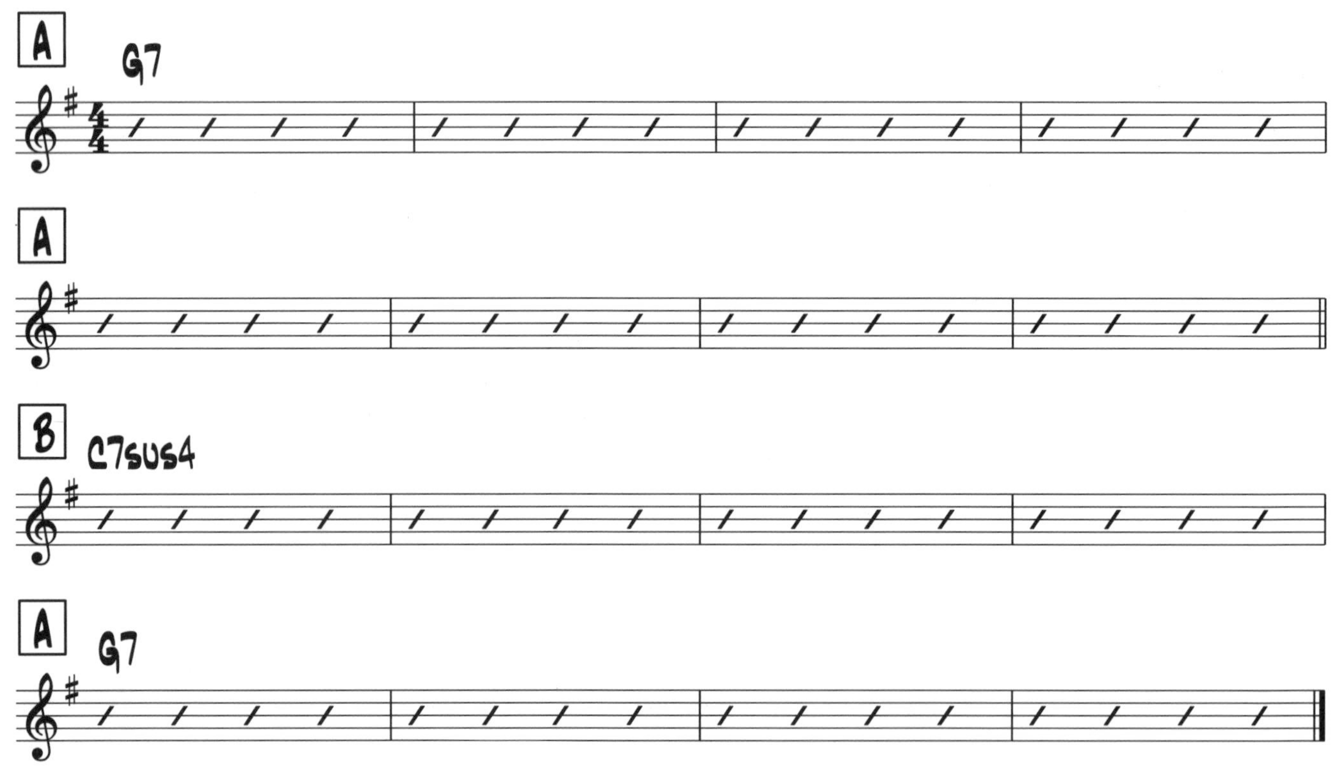

As you have already seen from practicing the comping patterns, there are two primary musical ideas in this tune. The sax plays contrasting melodies over them. Idea A is very sparse. It lasts for eight measures, with two phrases of sax melody. Idea B is in a more regular rhythm. It lasts for four measures. Then idea A returns for four measures. This form can be described simply as "AABA."

PRACTICE TIP

Imagine the melody as you play your comping part. This will help you keep your place—particularly during improvised solos, when nobody plays the melody. Although the form of this tune is simple, it is easy to get lost. The 4-measure return of idea A at the end of the form may be confused with the eight measures of idea A that begin the new chorus. Altogether, there are twelve measures of this idea, so keep careful count.

LISTEN 24 PLAY

Listen to the whole tune. Sing the melody while the saxophone plays the solo, and keep your place in the form. What is the arrangement on the recording? Is there an introduction or ending? Check your answer against the summary at the end of this chapter.

IDEAS FOR IMPROVISING: G MINOR AND MAJOR PENTATONIC

The G major pentatonic scale will work well for improvising on this tune's A section:

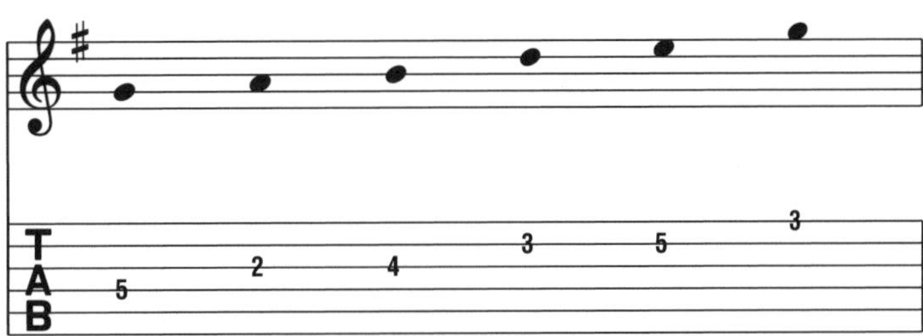

The G minor pentatonic scale will work well for improvising on this tune's B section:

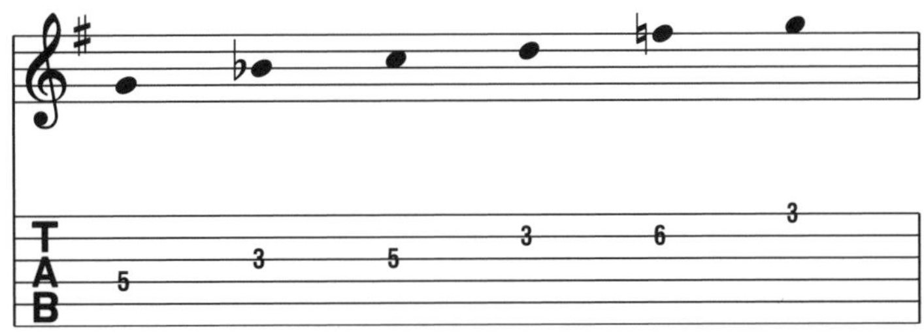

CALL AND RESPONSE

1. Echo each phrase, exactly as you hear it.
2. Improvise an answer to each phrase. Imitate the sound and rhythmic feel of the phase you hear, and use the notes from the G pentatonic scales.

LISTEN 27 PLAY

Listen

Play

G7

C7sus4

G7

LISTEN 28 PLAY

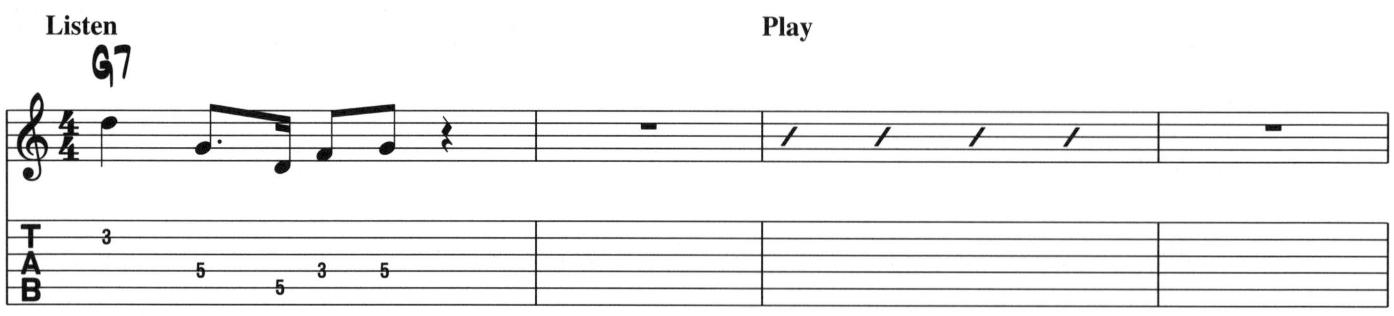

Write out a few of your own ideas. Use the G pentatonic scales.

LISTEN 29 PLAY

Create a one-chorus solo using any techniques you have learned. Memorize your solo and practice it along with the recording.

LESSON 20
READING

GUITAR PART

Play "Affordable" while reading from the guitar part.

LISTEN 29 PLAY

GUITAR PART

BY MATT MARVUGLIO

"LIGHT FUNK" ♩ = 84

INTRO

G7

MELODY

GUITAR

A

G7

A9

B♭/C

G7

TO CODA

B
SOLOS
G7
2
2
2
B9
Bb/C
G7
AFTER SOLOS, D.S. AL
2
CODA

LEAD SHEET

Play “Affordable” while reading the lead sheet.

AFFORDABLE

BY MATT MARVUGLIO

"LIGHT FUNK" ♩ = 84

G7

Bb/C

CHAPTER V
DAILY PRACTICE ROUTINE

PENTATONIC PRACTICE

Practice the G minor pentatonic scale starting on different notes. Play every note with a downstroke.

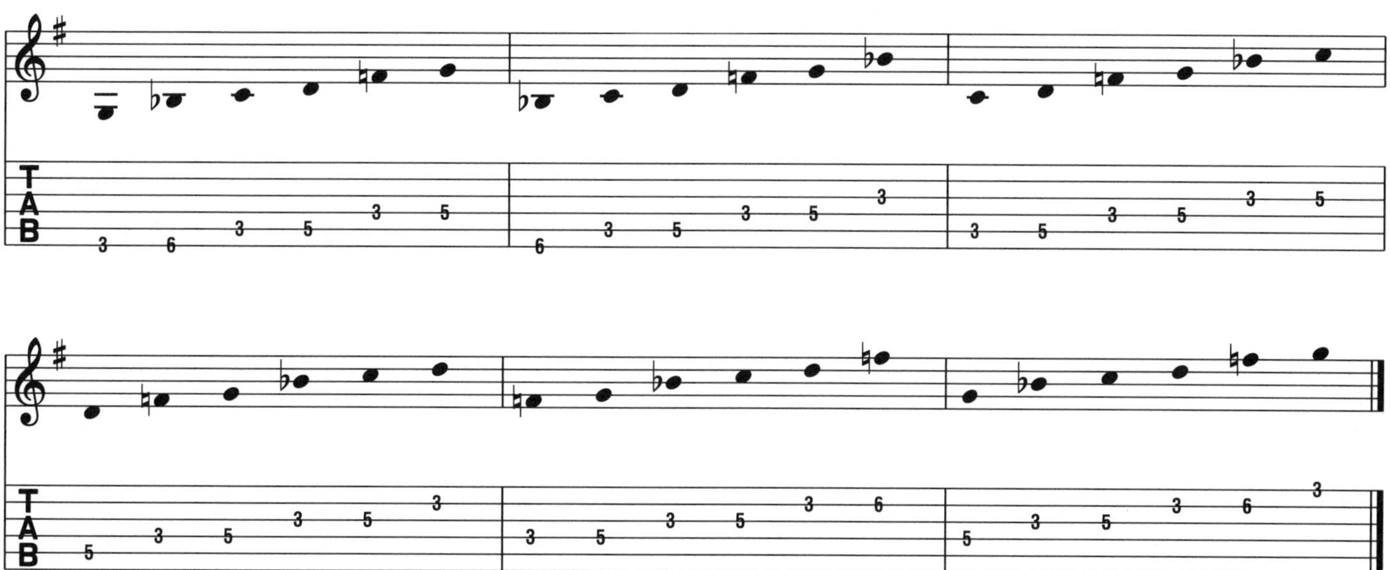

PICKING PRACTICE

Practice the following pickings on these licks.

CALL AND RESPONSE: LICKS

1. Echo each lick, exactly as you hear it.
2. Improvise an answer to each lick. Imitate the sound and rhythmic feel of the lick you hear, and use the notes from the G pentatonic scales. Try to imitate the articulations you hear on the recording.

Listen

Play

SOLO PRACTICE

Practice the following melody and play it with the first part to "Affordable." Hook into the groove's sixteenth-note feel.

LISTEN 29 PLAY

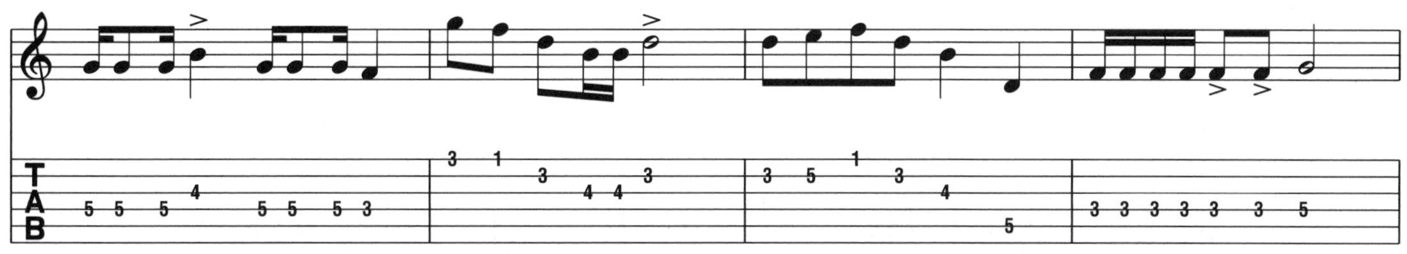

MEMORIZE

LISTEN 29 PLAY

Create your own comping part and improvised solo to "Affordable." Practice it along with the recording, and memorize it.

SUMMARY

FORM
16-BAR AABA
(1 CHORUS = 16 BARS)
A: 4 M.
B: 4 M.

ARRANGEMENT
INTRO: 8 M.
1 CHORUS MELODY
1 CHORUS SOLO
1 CHORUS MELODY

HARMONY
A G7 B Bb/C

SCALE
G MAJOR PENTATONIC
G MINOR PENTATONIC

PLAY "AFFORDABLE" WITH YOUR OWN BAND!

PLAYING HARD ROCK — CHAPTER VI

"Don't Look Down" is a *hard rock* tune. Hard rock first appeared in the late 1960s. It has characteristic heavy bass, long, drawn-out chords, and amplified instruments. To hear more hard rock, listen to artists such as Aerosmith, Metallica, Powerman 5000, the Allman Brothers Band, Rob Zombie, Godsmack, 311, Stone Temple Pilots, Black Crowes, Steve Vai, and Smashing Pumpkins.

LESSON 21
TECHNIQUE/THEORY

Listen to "Don't Look Down," and then play along with the recording. Try to match the guitar part. This tune has two parts.

LISTEN 31 PLAY

In the first part, the guitar doubles the sax melody (head only):

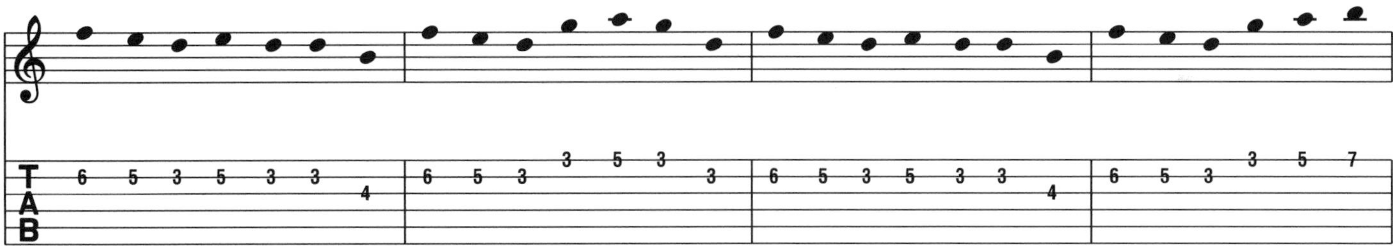

During solos, in the first part, the guitar doubles the bass riff:

In the second part, the guitar plays power chords along with the bass:

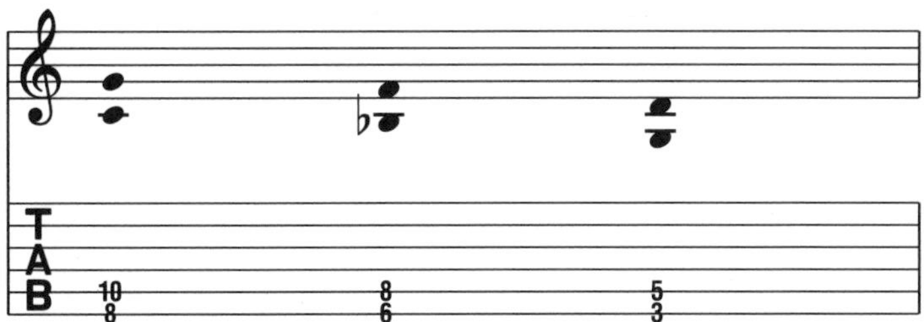

MELODY

LISTEN 31 PLAY

Play this melody in third position (first finger on the third fret). Stretch your fourth finger to the seventh fret to reach the last note B, but keep your hand in third position. Play along with the recording and try to match the guitar.

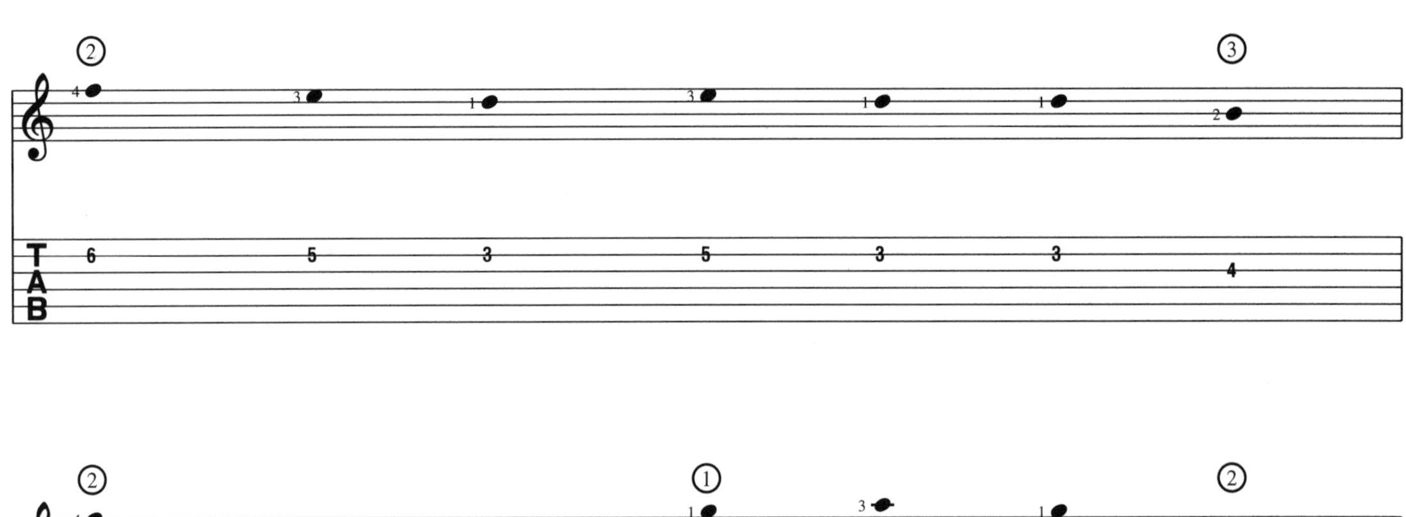

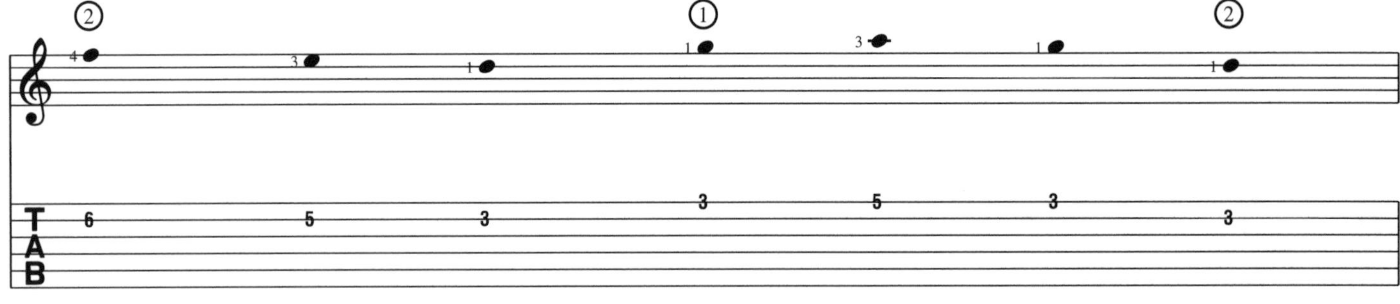

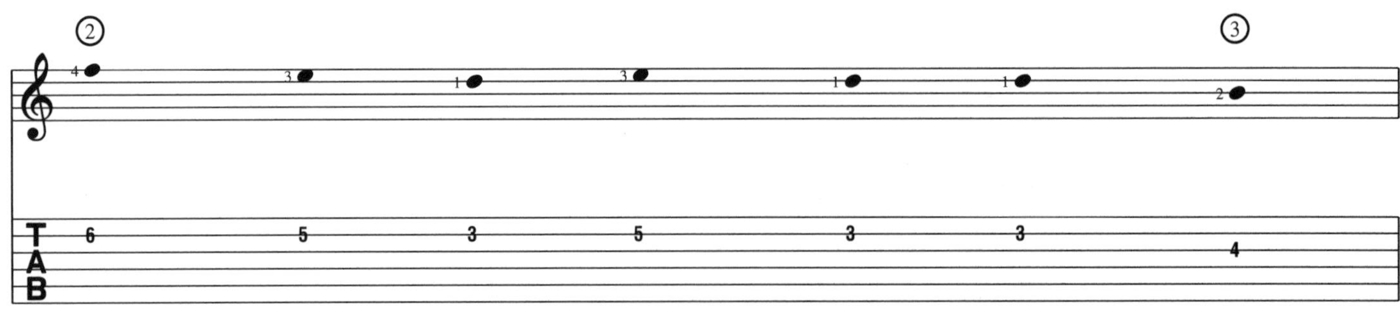

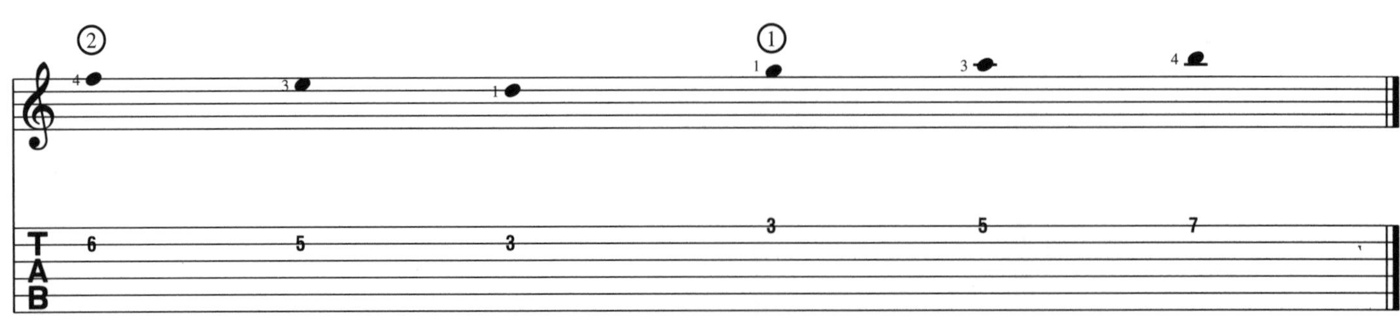

BACKGROUND RIFFS

First Riff

LISTEN 32 PLAY

Listen to the first part. Follow your ear, and imitate the guitar/bass part, taking turns playing the riff with the recording. Play all notes on the sixth string in first position.

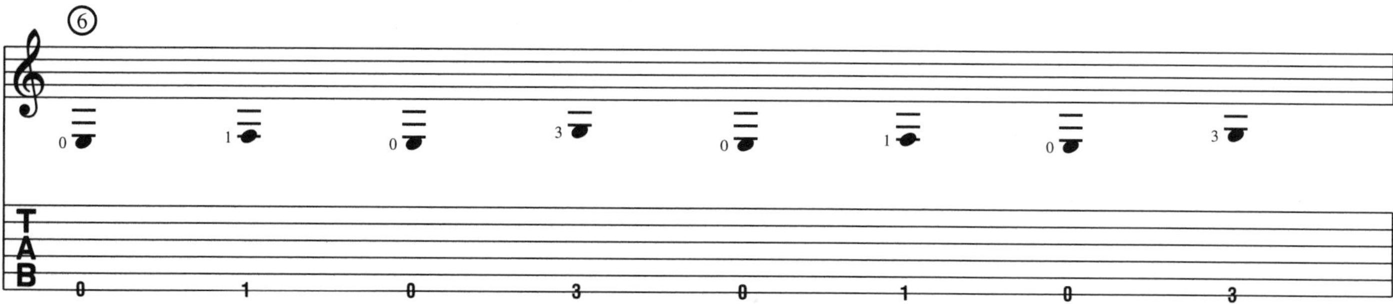

Second Riff

LISTEN 33 PLAY

Listen to the second part. Follow your ear and play along as you did with the first riff. The guitar plays power chords, using the fifth and sixth strings, as in the other rock tune, "Sweet." Practice this power chord pattern until you can play it easily.

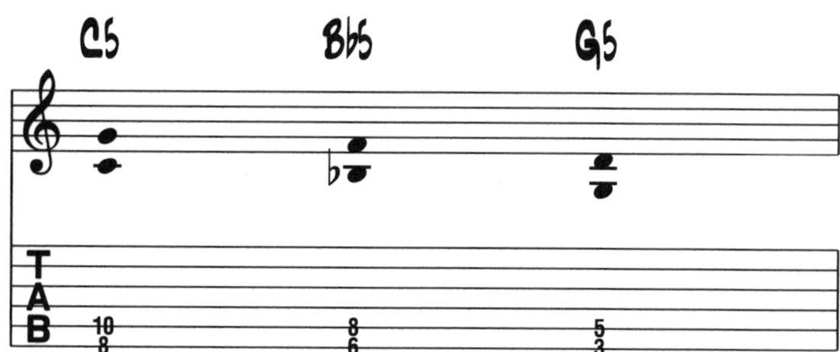

Alternate between the two riffs.

LESSON 22
LEARNING THE GROOVE

HOOKING UP TO HARD ROCK

Listen to "Don't Look Down." This tune has a standard rock/metal groove. It is a heavy feel, with very simple drum and bass parts. These parts must be simple because they are intended to be played in large arenas, where echoes would make busier parts sound muddy. It's a case of "less is more."

During the solos, the guitar doubles the bass, playing power chords in the second part. Doubling the bass is very common in hard rock.

Listen to the first part to "Don't Look Down." Find the pulse, and strum dampened strings on the backbeat, along with the snare drum hits.

LISTEN 32 PLAY

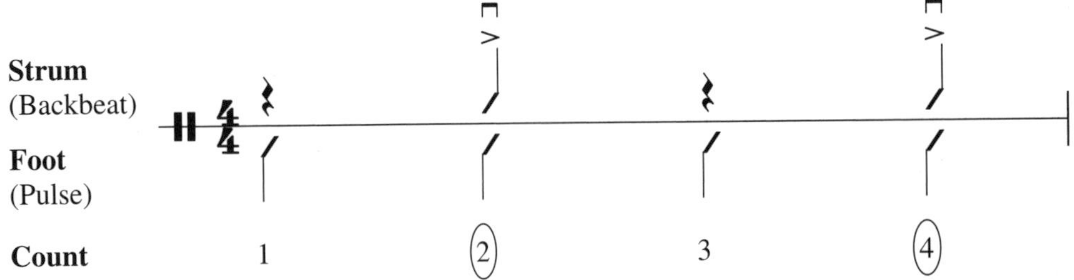

Tap the quarter-note pulse with your foot, strum the backbeat, and count the sixteenths. When you are ready, do this along with the recording.

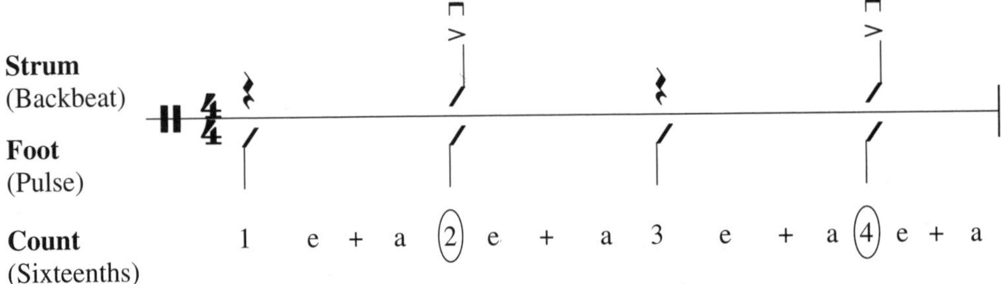

LEARNING "DON'T LOOK DOWN"

Play the rhythms of the first riff. Accent the syncopation. When you are ready, strum along with the recording.

LISTEN 32 PLAY

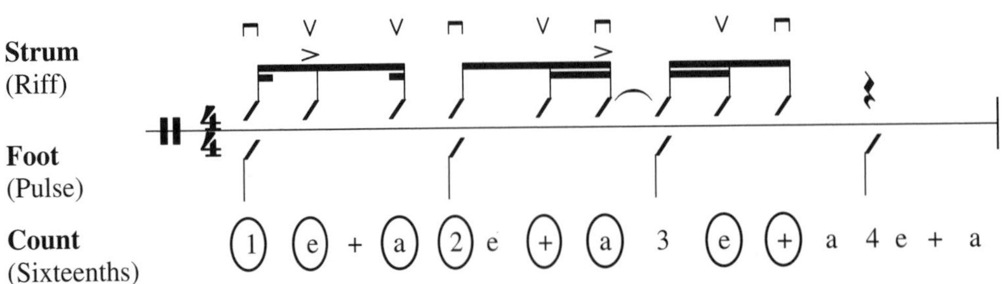

Play the riff to "Don't Look Down" along with the recording. Count the sixteenths, and try to match the rhythmic feel of the keyboard and guitar on the recording. Accent the syncopations. Use all downstrokes to get a hard-edged rock sound.

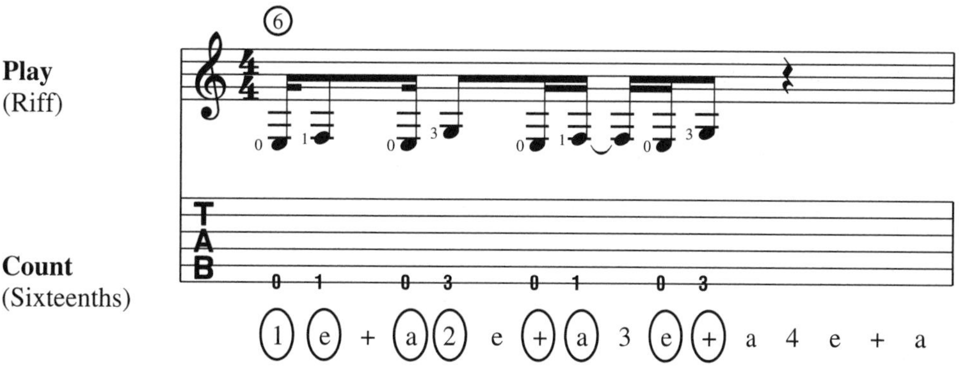

The second part also has a syncopation. Play the rhythms to the second riff of "Don't Look Down," and accent the syncopated note.

LISTEN 33 PLAY

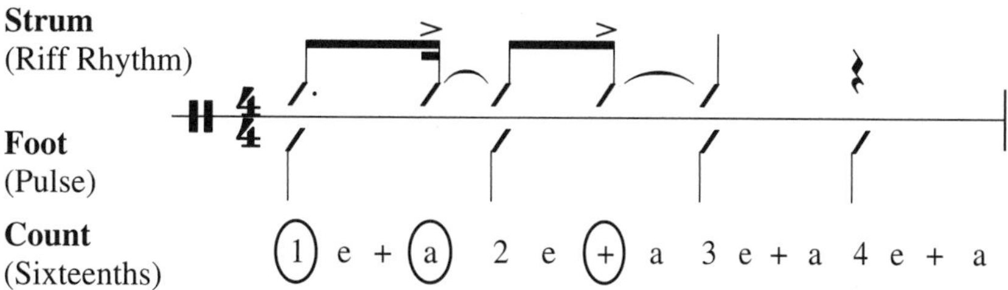

Play the second riff. While you play these power chords, use all down strokes, count the sixteenths, and hook up with the groove.

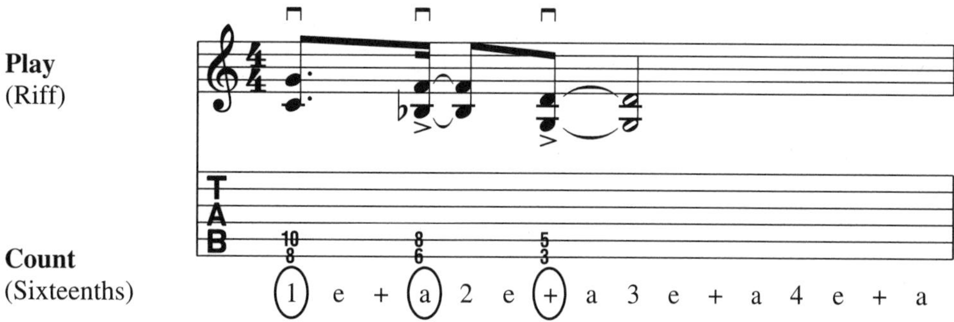

LESSON 23
IMPROVISATION

FORM AND ARRANGEMENT

Listen to the recording and try to figure out the form and arrangement by ear. How long does each section of the form last? Is there an introduction or ending? For how many measures or beats does each chord last? Write down as much information as you can. Check your answers against the summary at the end of this chapter.

This tune has a 20-bar AB form. Part A has an active riff that builds a lot of tension. It lasts for sixteen measures. Part B is less active than the first part. It lasts for four measures. There is a 4-measure introduction at the beginning of the tune. It comes from the B section.

LISTEN 31 PLAY

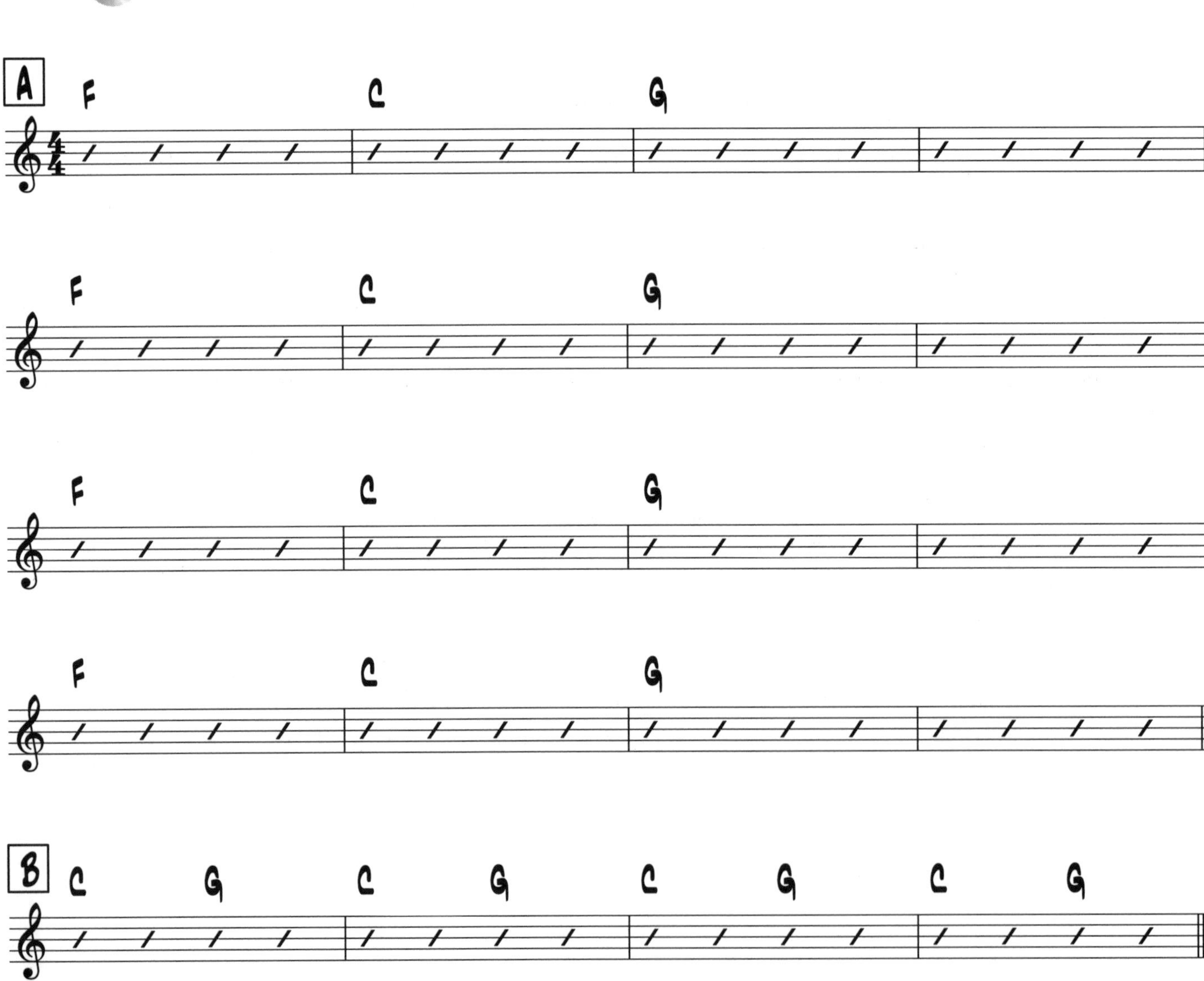

IDEAS FOR IMPROVISING: G MINOR AND MAJOR PENTATONIC

The G major pentatonic scale will work well for improvising on this tune's A section:

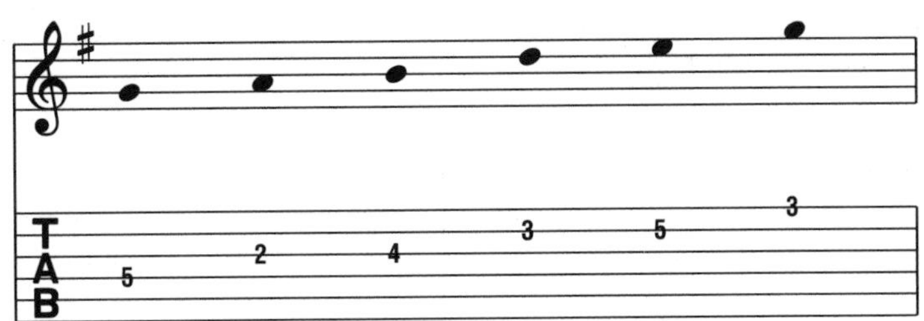

The G minor pentatonic scale will work well for improvising on this tune's B section:

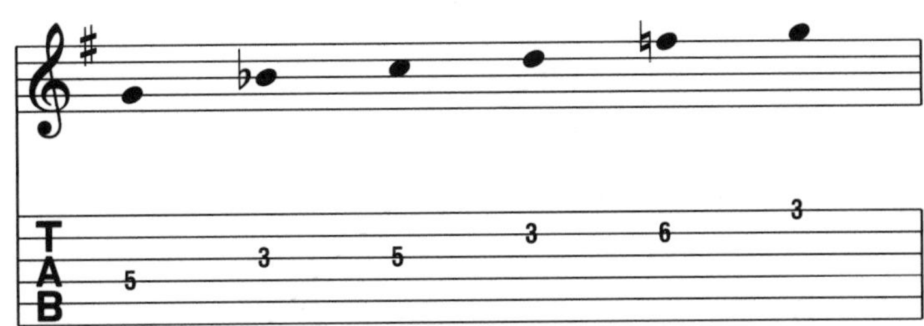

Practice both these scales. You can use both of them when you improvise, depending on the chord.

LISTEN 31 PLAY

Listen again to "Don't Look Down," and play along with the melody. Notice the B-natural at the end of each 4-measure phrase.

CALL AND RESPONSE

1. Echo each phrase, exactly as you hear it.
2. Improvise an answer to each phrase. Imitate the sound and rhythmic feel of the phrase you hear, and use the notes from the G pentatonic scales.

LISTEN 34 PLAY

Write out a few of your own ideas.

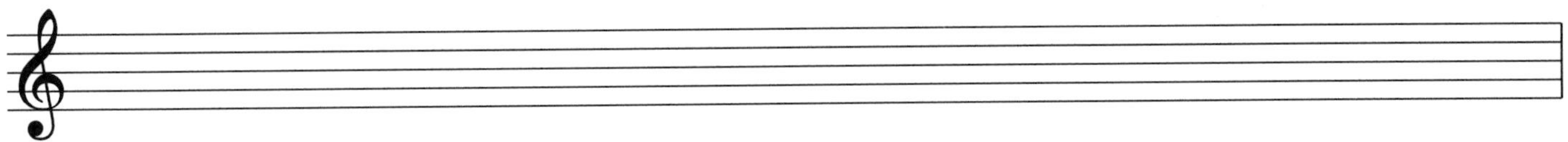

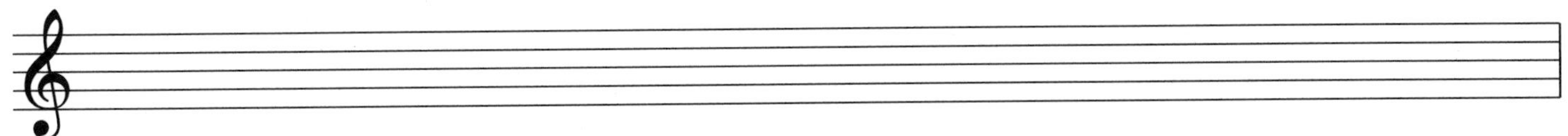

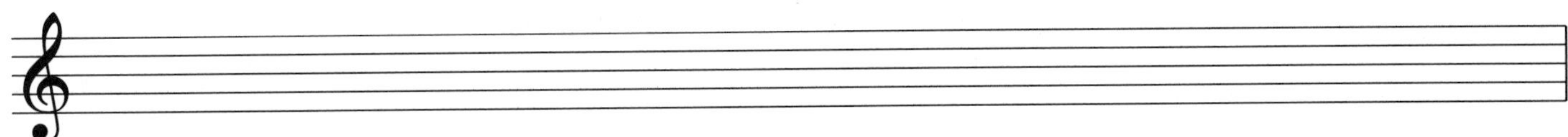

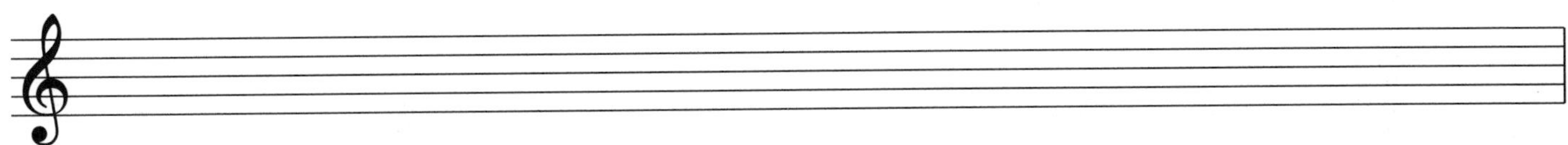

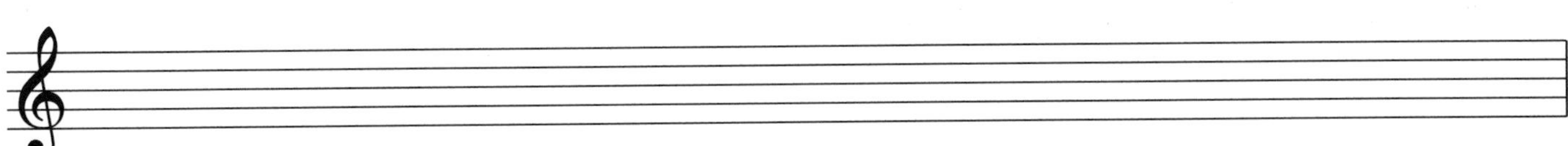

LISTEN 35 PLAY

Create a one-chorus solo using any techniques you have learned. Memorize your solo and practice it with the recording.

LESSON 24
READING

GUITAR PART

Play "Don't Look Down" along with the recording. Use the written guitar part.

1. 2. :‖ — First and second ending markings. The first time you play these measures, play the *first ending*—the measures under the number 1. Then return to the begin-repeat sign (‖:). The second time you play these measures, skip the first ending and play the *second ending*—the measures under the number 2. Then, continue through the rest of the form.

LISTEN 35 PLAY

2.
A17
G
C
G
To Coda
B
Solos
F
C
G
F
C
G
B17
C
G
After solos, D.S. al
Coda
G

LEAD SHEET

Play your own part to "Don't Look Down" and follow along with the lead sheet.

LISTEN 35 PLAY

By Matt Marvuglio

"Hard Rock" ♩ = 88

Intro

C G C G C G C G

A

F C G

F C G

F C G

F C G

B

C G C G C G C G

Ending

G Unison: bass, keys & guitar

PERFORMANCE TIP

When you play from a lead sheet, use it to help you keep your place. Even when you keep repeating the same comping patterns, follow along with the melody and chords as they are played by other instruments.

CHAPTER VI
DAILY PRACTICE ROUTINE

CHORD FORMS AND MELODY

The rhythm guitar part on this recording doubles the melody and bass, but you may want to play comping chords instead—particularly if your band has more than one guitarist.

As you saw on the lead sheet, the A section of "Don't Look Down" has three chords—F, C, and G. Here are some basic forms of these chords:

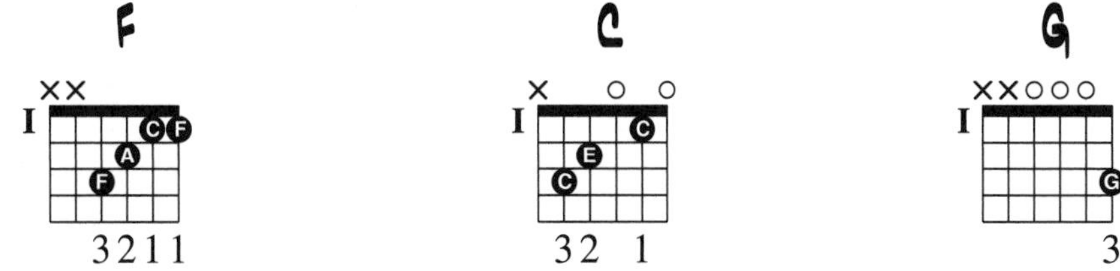

You may use these chord forms in your comping part. However, a better choice would be to use chord forms that take their highest notes *from the melody*, as you will see next.

Listen to keyboard's chords on the recording. Notice that most of the highest notes of its chords double the melody notes (played by the guitar and sax).

Here is the first melodic phrase of "Don't Look Down":

This melody uses chord tones on prominent beats: F is the root of the F chord, E is the third of the C chord, and D is the fifth of the G chord. This makes it easy to choose chord forms that will sound good with the melody.

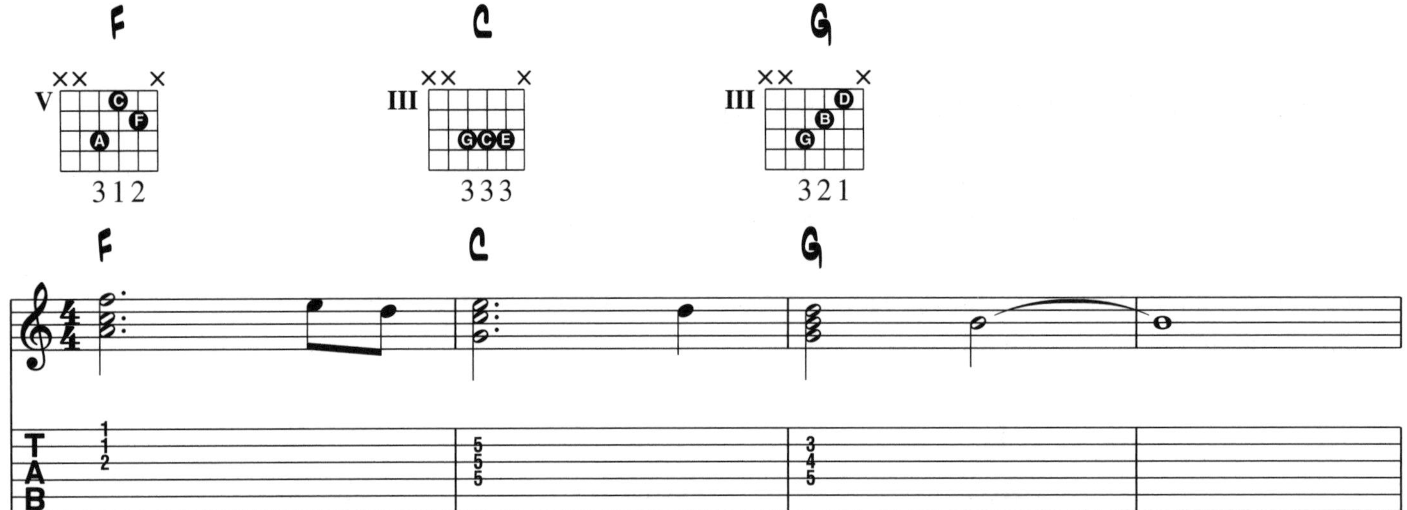

LISTEN 35 PLAY

Practice these chord forms until you can switch from one to the other easily. Then create a comping part to "Don't Look Down." Play it with the recording.

PERFORMANCE TIP

The top notes of chords are very important because they draw the listeners ear. When you choose a chord form, think carefully about the top note. It should be in the melody or sound good when played along with the melody.

RHYTHM PRACTICE

Rock grooves have a sixteenth-note feel, as you first saw in "Sweet." Play this exercise slowly, on muted strings, and keep a steady beat. Make sure that beats 2 and 4 are strong in every bar.

IDEAS FOR IMPROVISATION: CHORD TONES

Chord tones will sound great in a solo to "Don't Look Down" because of the strong chord motion, and because the written melody features chord tones so prominently.

Here are the chord tones in a register that will work well for your solo. Use just the first, second, and third strings.

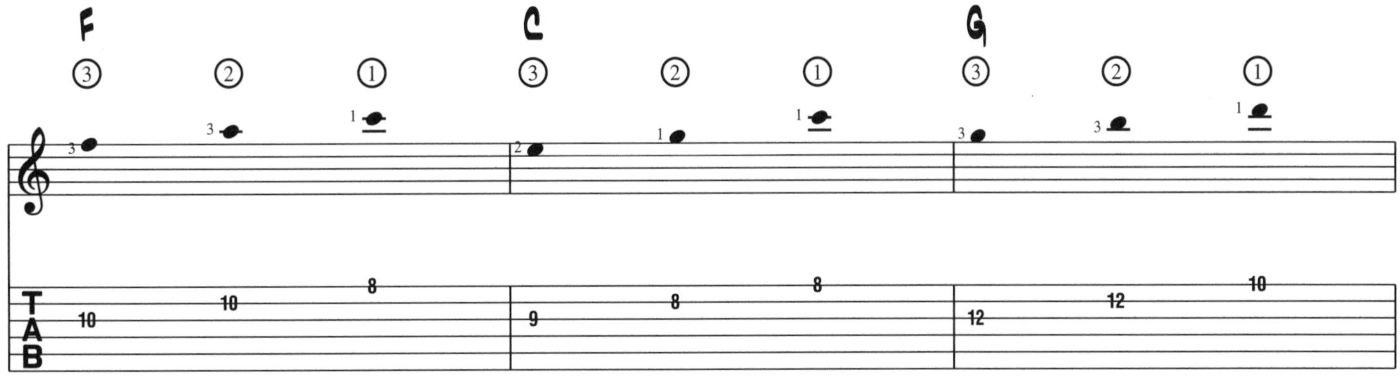

SOLO PRACTICE

Practice the following melody and play it with the first part to "Don't Look Down." Hook into the groove's sixteenth note feel.

MEMORIZE

LISTEN 35 PLAY

Create your own comping part and improvised solo to "Don't Look Down." Practice it along with the recording, and memorize it.

SUMMARY

FORM
20-BAR AB FORM
(1 CHORUS = 20 BARS)
A: 16 M.
B: 4 M.

ARRANGEMENT
INTRO: 4 M.
1 CHORUS MELODY
1 CHORUS SOLO
1 CHORUS MELODY
END: 2 M.

HARMONY
F C G

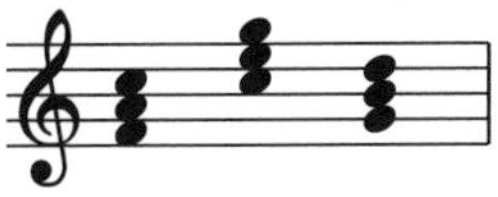

SCALE
G MAJOR PENTATONIC
G MINOR PENTATONIC

PLAY "DON'T LOOK DOWN" WITH YOUR OWN BAND!

PLAYING BOSSA NOVA — CHAPTER VII

"Take Your Time" is a *bossa nova* tune. Bossa nova began in Brazil, combining American jazz and an Afro-Brazilian form of dance music called *samba*. To hear more bossa nova, listen to Stan Getz, Antonio Carlos Jobim, Eliane Elias, Astrud Gilberto, Flora Purim, Dave Valentine, and Spyro Gyra.

LESSON 25
TECHNIQUE/THEORY

Listen to "Take Your Time" on the recording. The guitar plays the melody at the head and comps chords during the solos.

LISTEN 36 PLAY

Here is the melody:

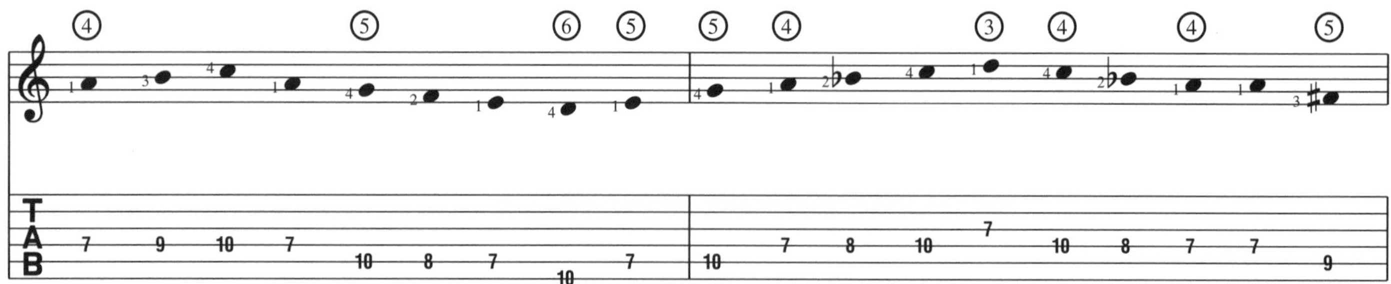

Here are the chords:

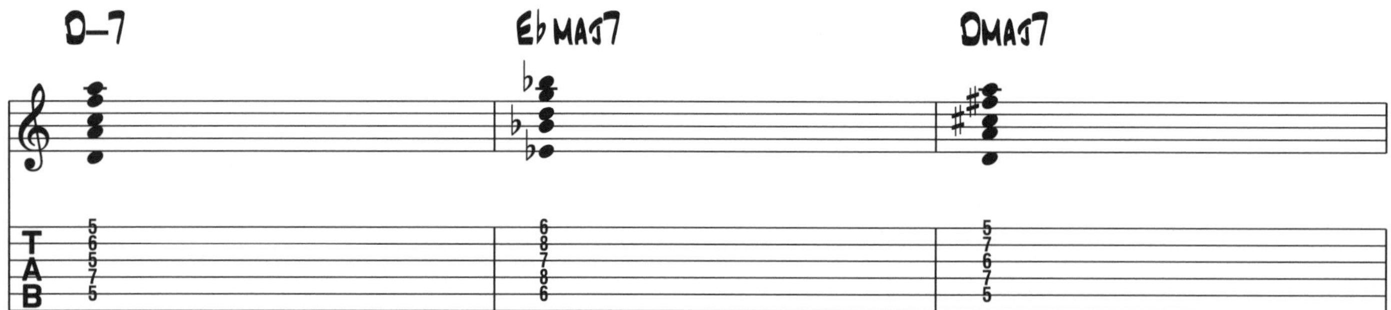

LEGATO

The melody to "Take Your Time" is played very *legato*—notes are held long, and connected together smoothly. Each note rings all the way up to the next note.

Hand Position

To play legato, keep your left-hand fingers pressed against the fretboard until you are ready to change notes. This becomes easier with practice, as you develop left-hand strength.

Practice the melody to "Take Your Time," and match the phrasing played by the guitar and sax. Hold the notes for as long as they sound on the recording.

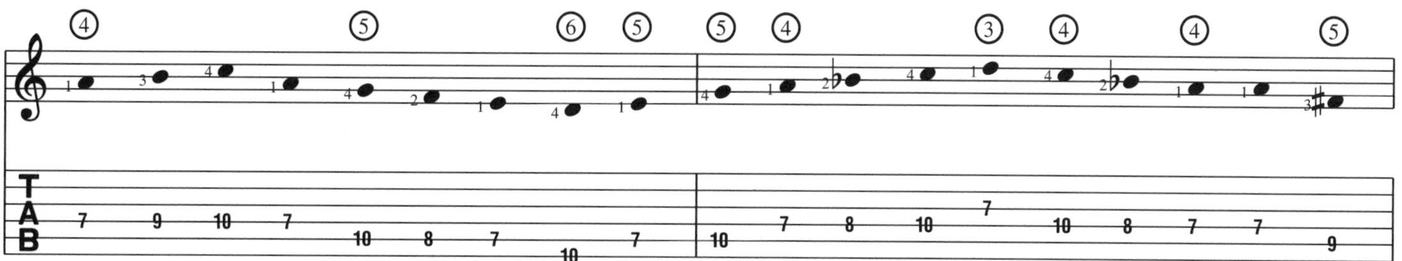

PRACTICE TIP

Play this melody in seventh position so that you can avoid open strings, which are more difficult to mute. Watch out for the B♭ and F♯ in the second half of the melody.

COMPING CHORDS

LISTEN 36 PLAY

The rhythm guitar part to "Take Your Time" has three chords:

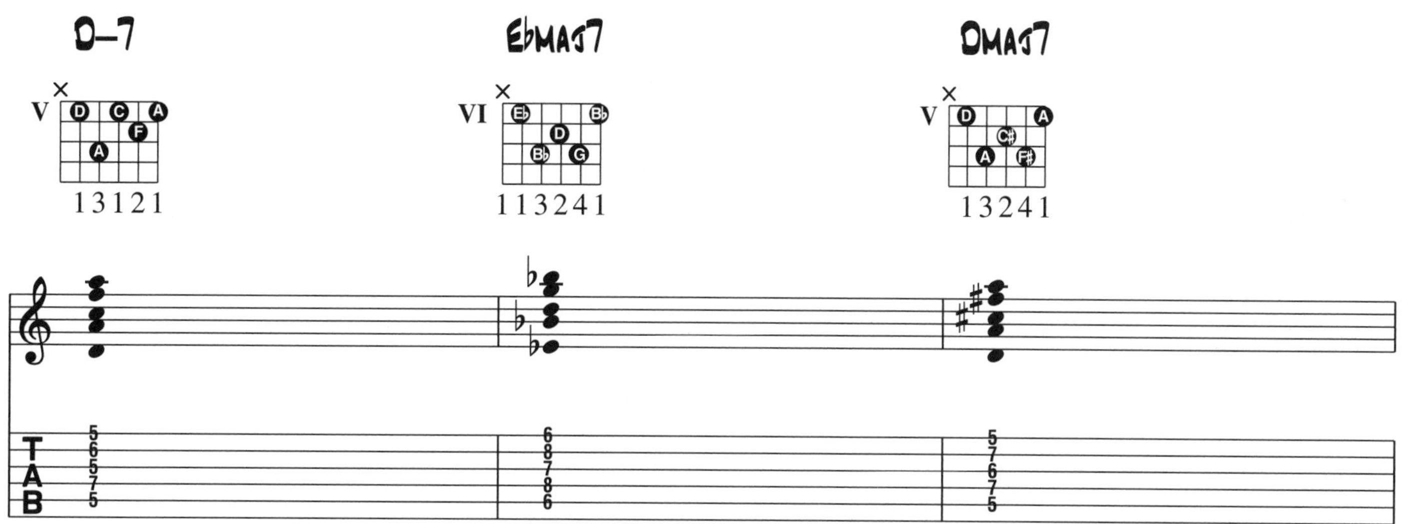

D–7 and DMAJ7 are played in fifth position. E♭MAJ7 is played in sixth position. E♭MAJ7 and DMAJ7 use the same hand position, so you really only need to learn two chord forms.

The key to switching between these chords is first practicing D–7 to DMAJ7. Notice their similarities; only two notes change (C and F move to C♯ and F♯).

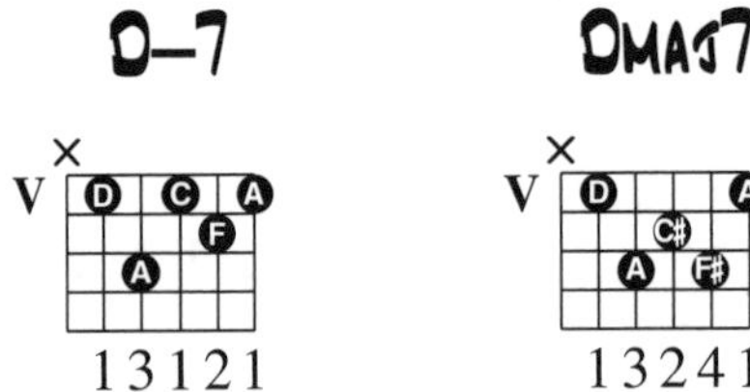

First, play D–7. To change to DMAJ7, your first and third fingers stay in the same place. Move your second finger to the third string, sixth fret, and add your fourth finger to the second string, seventh fret.

Chord Practice

Practice moving between D–7, DMAJ7, and E♭MAJ7.

D–7	DMAJ7	D–7	DMAJ7		
DMAJ7	E♭MAJ7	DMAJ7	E♭MAJ7		
D–7	DMAJ7	E♭MAJ7	D–7	DMAJ7	E♭MAJ7
D–7	E♭MAJ7	DMAJ7	D–7	E♭MAJ7	DMAJ7

LISTEN 37 PLAY

Play the chords in time, along with the recording.

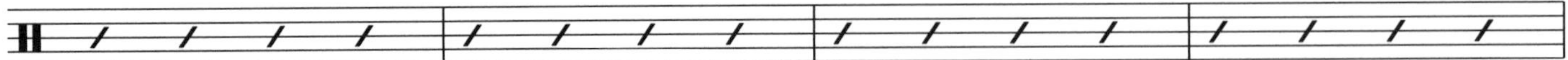

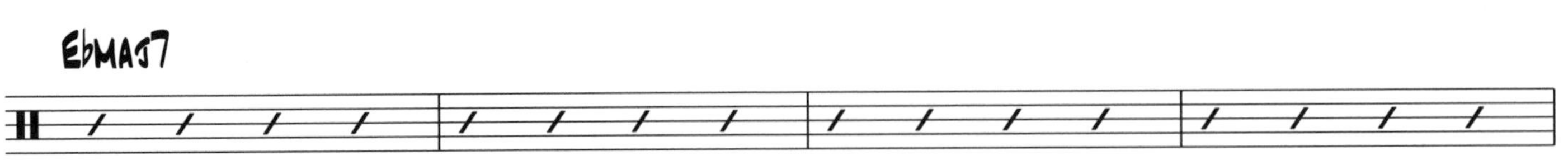

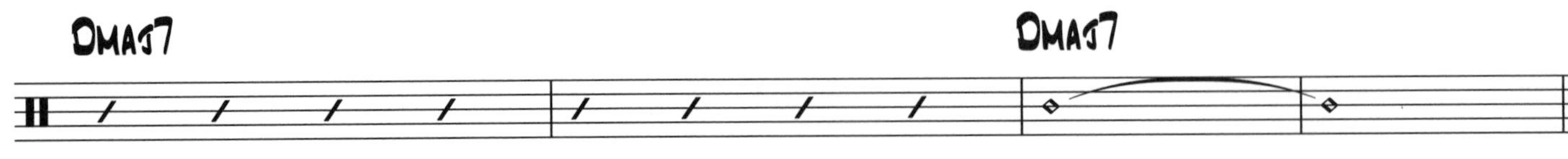

Hold

LESSON 26
LEARNING THE GROOVE

HOOKING UP TO BOSSA NOVA

Listen to "Take Your Time." This tune is a bossa nova, a style of music that originated in Brazil. Throughout the tune, a two-bar rhythmic pattern repeats. This repeating pattern is an essential part of bossa nova. The drum plays it on a rim-click.

Repeating rhythmic structures are at the heart of much African-based music, including Afro-Caribbean and most South and Latin American styles.

LISTEN 37 PLAY

Listen to "Take Your Time." Bossa nova (sometimes just called *bossa*) has a straight eighth-note feel, with many syncopations. Find the pulse, and strum dampened strings on the backbeat.

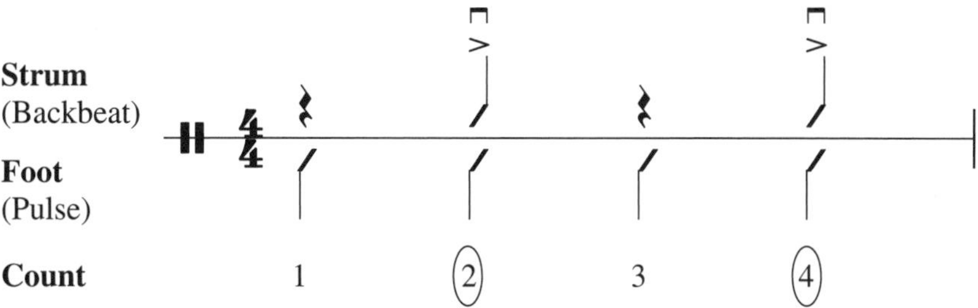

Tap the quarter-note pulse with your foot, strum the backbeat, and count the eighths. When you are ready, do this along with the recording.

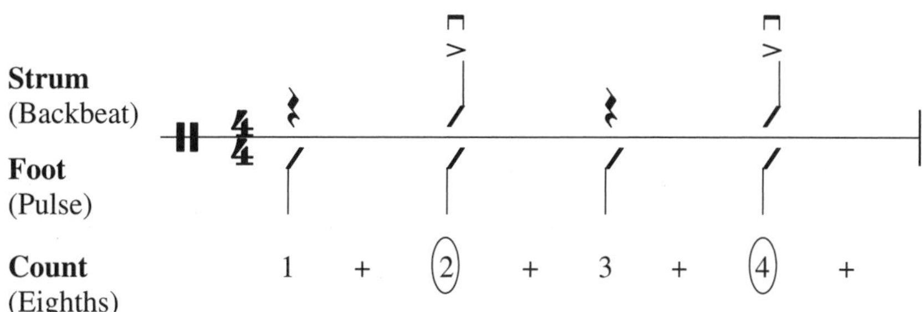

LEARNING "TAKE YOUR TIME"

Play the comping rhythms to "Take Your Time," and accent the syncopation. When you are ready, play along with the recording.

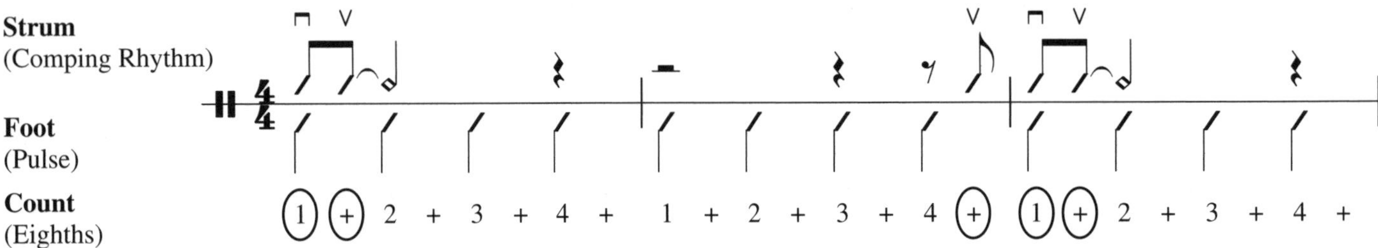

Play the written comping part. While you play, count the eighths, and hook up with the groove.

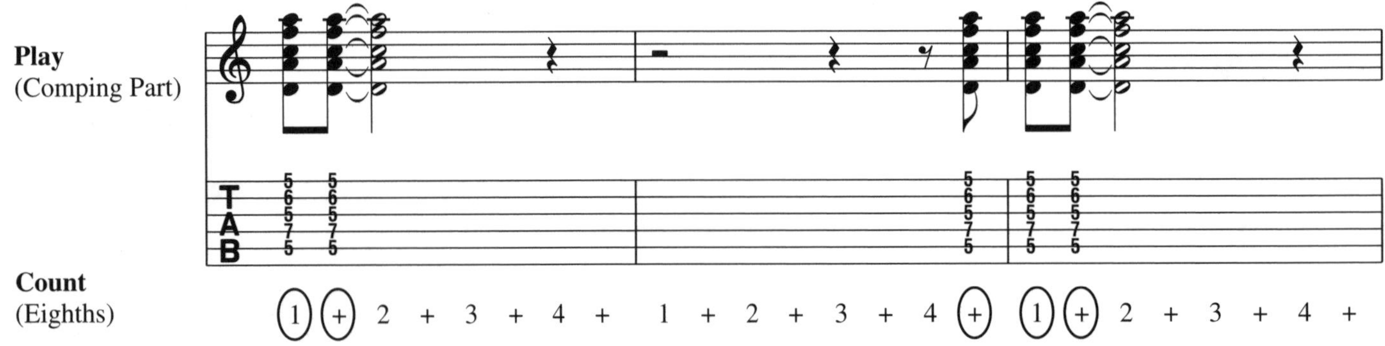

LESSON 27
IMPROVISATION

Listen to "Take Your Time" and try to figure out the form and arrangement by ear. Then continue with this chapter.

FORM AND ARRANGEMENT

This tune follows a 16-bar AB form. Each phrase of the melody lasts for eight measures.

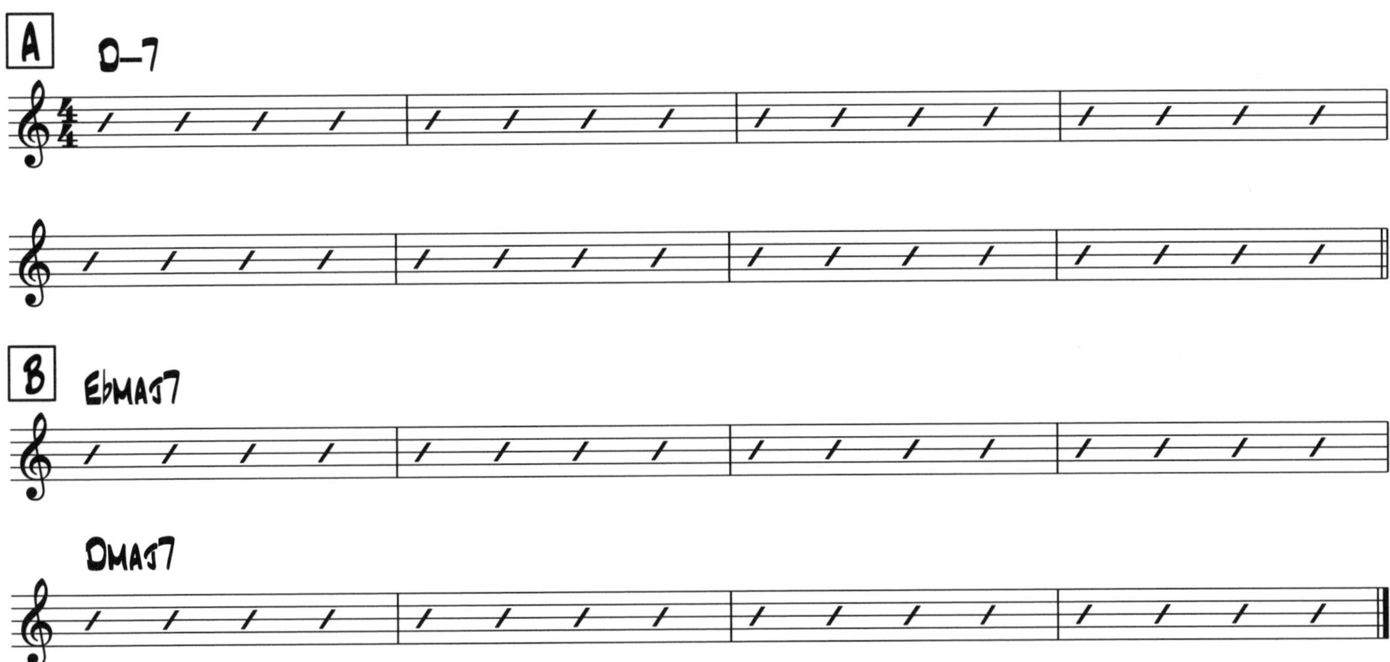

What is the arrangement on the recording? Figure it out by ear, and then check your answer against the summary at the end of this chapter.

IDEAS FOR IMPROVISING: PENTATONIC SCALES

For the first twelve measures of this tune (over the D–7 and E♭MAJ7 chords) we will use the D minor pentatonic scale to improvise. Practice this scale in two octaves.

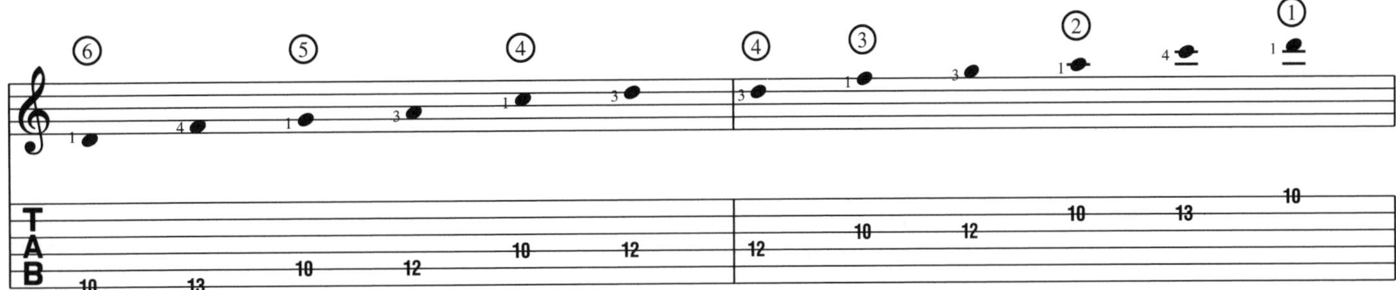

In the last four measures, over the DMA7 chord, solo using notes from the D major pentatonic scale. Major pentatonic scales work well when improvising on major or major-7 chords.

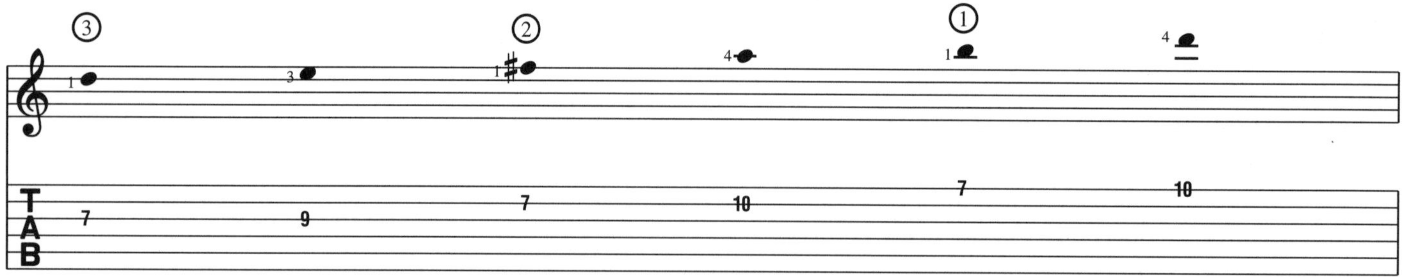

PENTATONIC PRACTICE

Practice the D major and minor pentatonic scales along with the recording. Notice the differences in their sounds, and how D minor pentatonic sounds against D–7 versus E♭MA7.

LISTEN 37 PLAY

D Minor Pentatonic

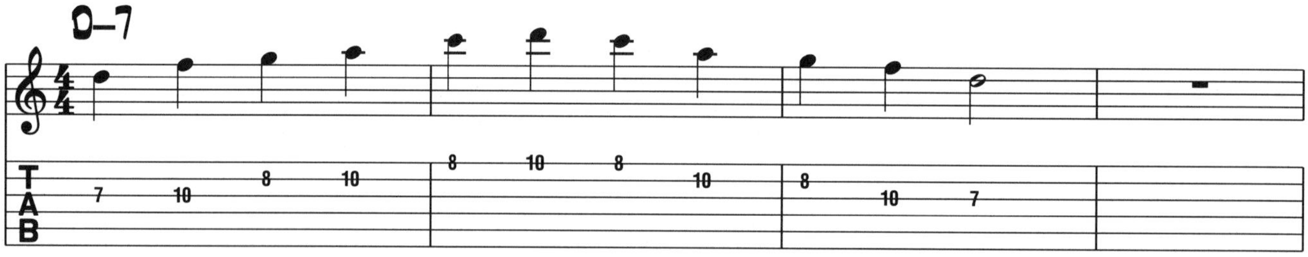

D–7

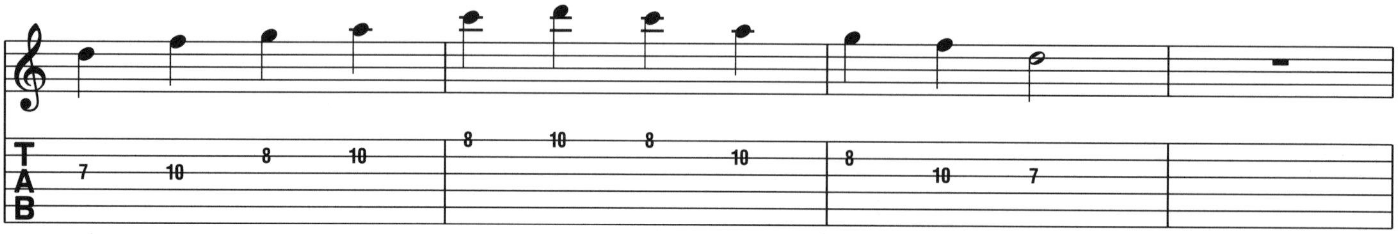

D Minor Pentatonic

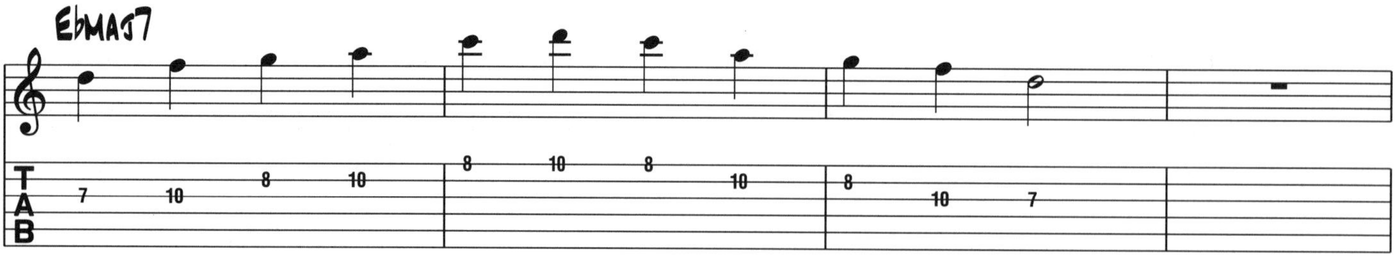

E♭MA7

D Major Pentatonic

DMA7

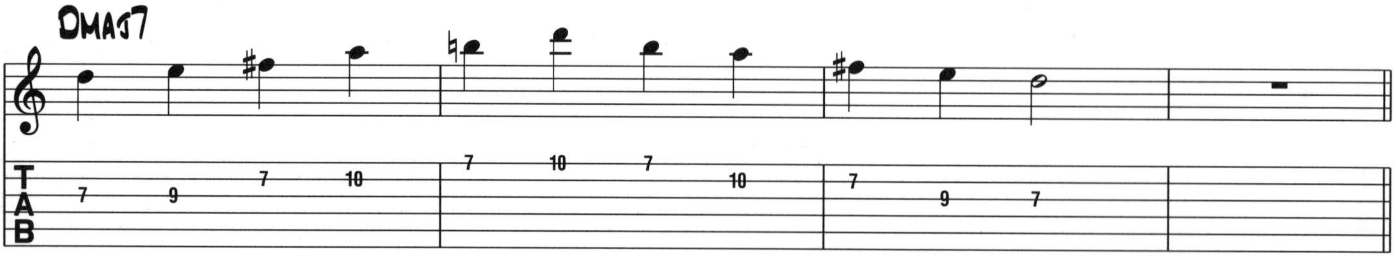

CALL AND RESPONSE

1. Echo each phrase, exactly as you hear it.
2. Improvise an answer to each phrase. Imitate the sound and rhythmic feel of the phrase you hear, and use the notes from the D pentatonic scales.

LISTEN 38 PLAY

Write out some of your own ideas. Use notes from the D pentatonic scales.

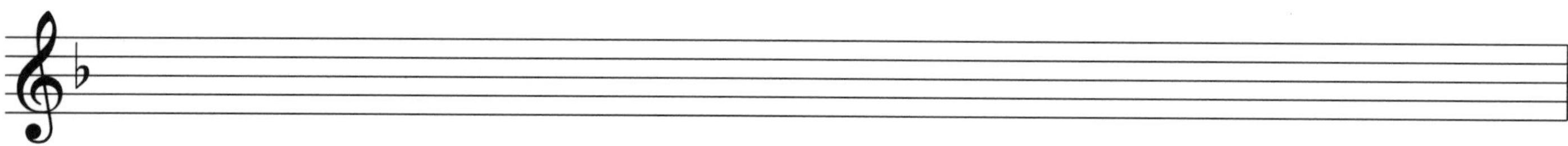

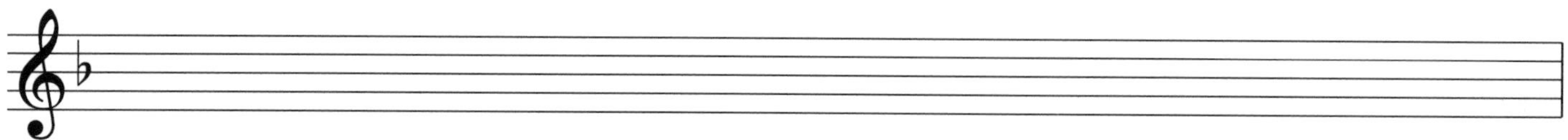

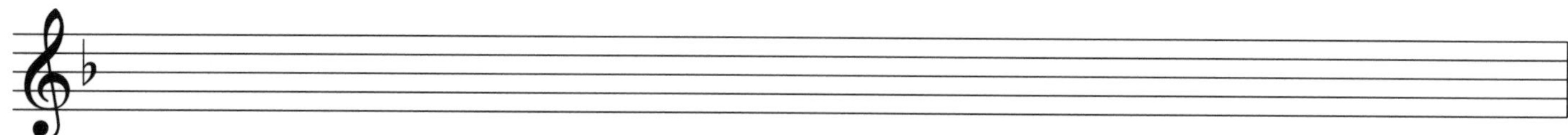

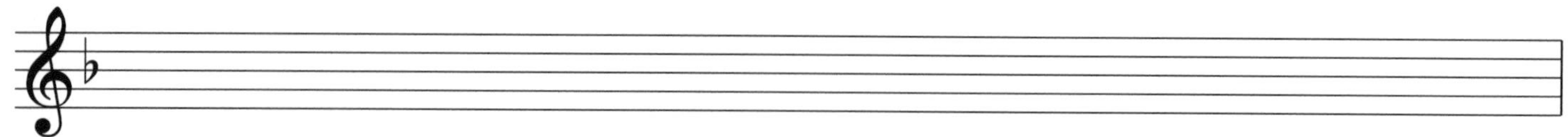

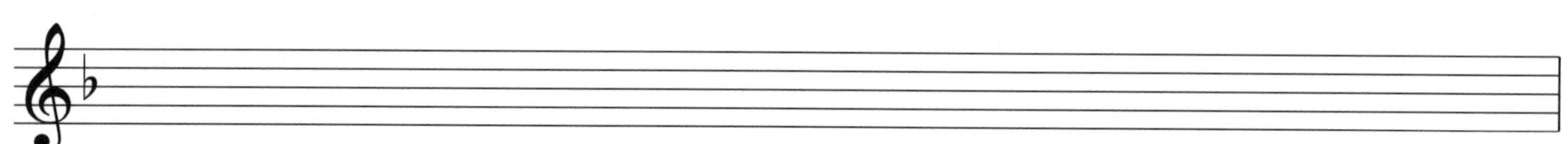

LISTEN 39 PLAY

Create a one-chorus solo using any techniques you have learned. Memorize your solo and practice it along with the recording.

LESSON 28
READING

GUITAR PART

2 Two-measure repeat. Repeat the previously notated two measures.

Play "Take Your Time" and use the written part.

LISTEN 39 PLAY

LEAD SHEET

Play "Take Your Time" and follow the lead sheet, using your own comping part.

Take Your Time

By Matt Marvuglio

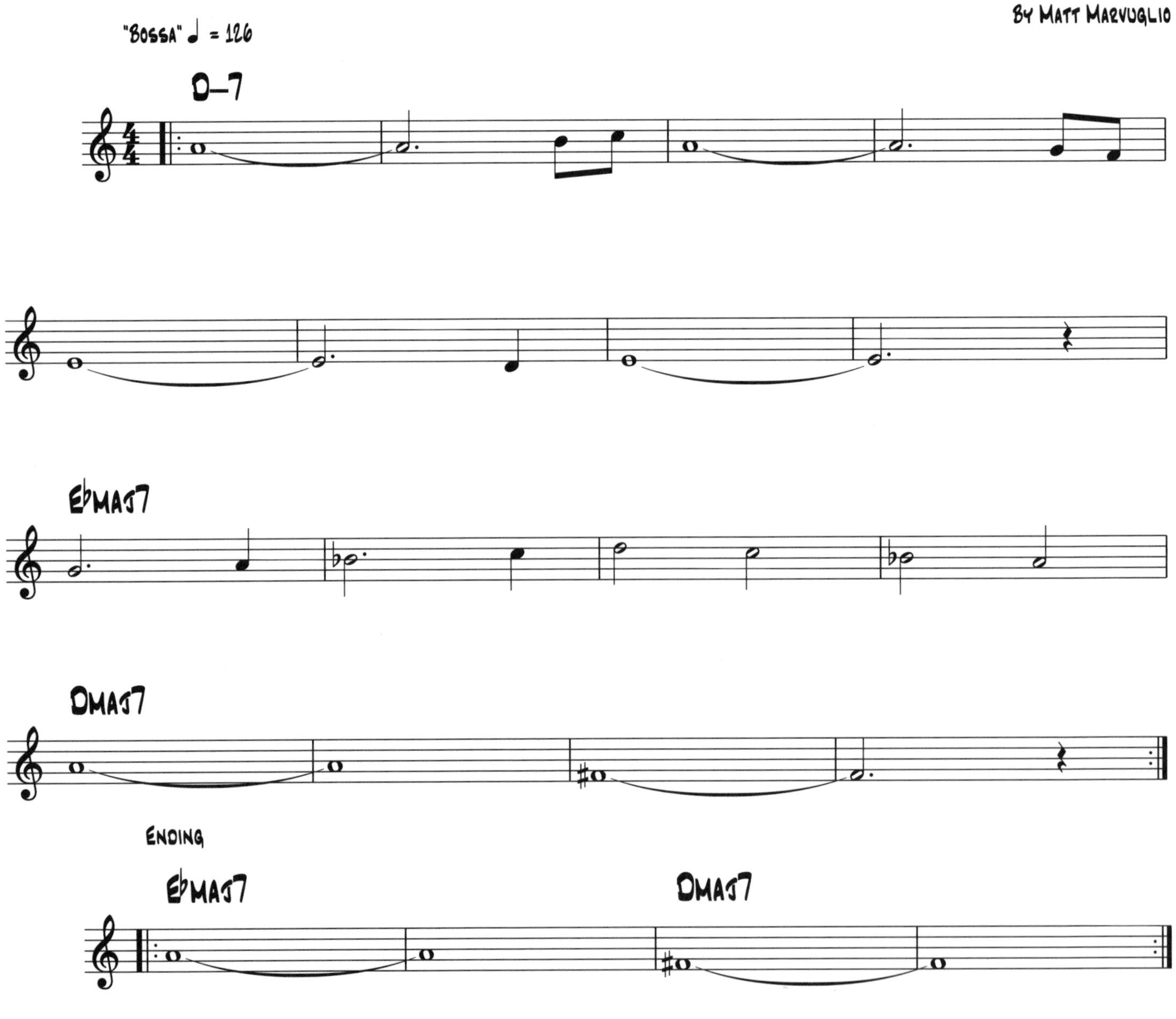

"Bossa" ♩ = 126

D–7

E♭MAJ7

DMAJ7

Ending

E♭MAJ7

DMAJ7

CHAPTER VII
DAILY PRACTICE ROUTINE

MOVABLE CHORD FORMS

If a chord form has no open strings, it is *movable*—the same fingering can be moved to different frets to play different chords.

Bossa nova often has rich guitar chords, with low roots on the fifth and sixth strings. Here are two chord forms that would work well in bossa nova and other styles that use full-sounding guitar chords.

First, here is a chord form for major chords, with the root on the fifth string. D major is shown:

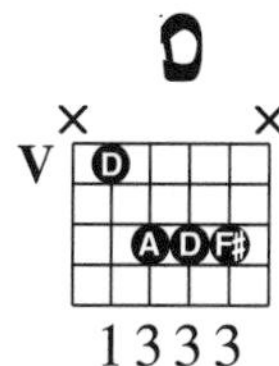

The next chord form uses all six strings, with the root on the sixth string. D major is shown again:

Practice these chord forms on every fret, up and down the fingerboard.

MORE ABOUT CHORDS

Root on Fifth String

Small changes to the major chord forms result in other kinds of chords. Practice these chord forms, beginning on C major. Then move them up and down the fingerboard to every fret.

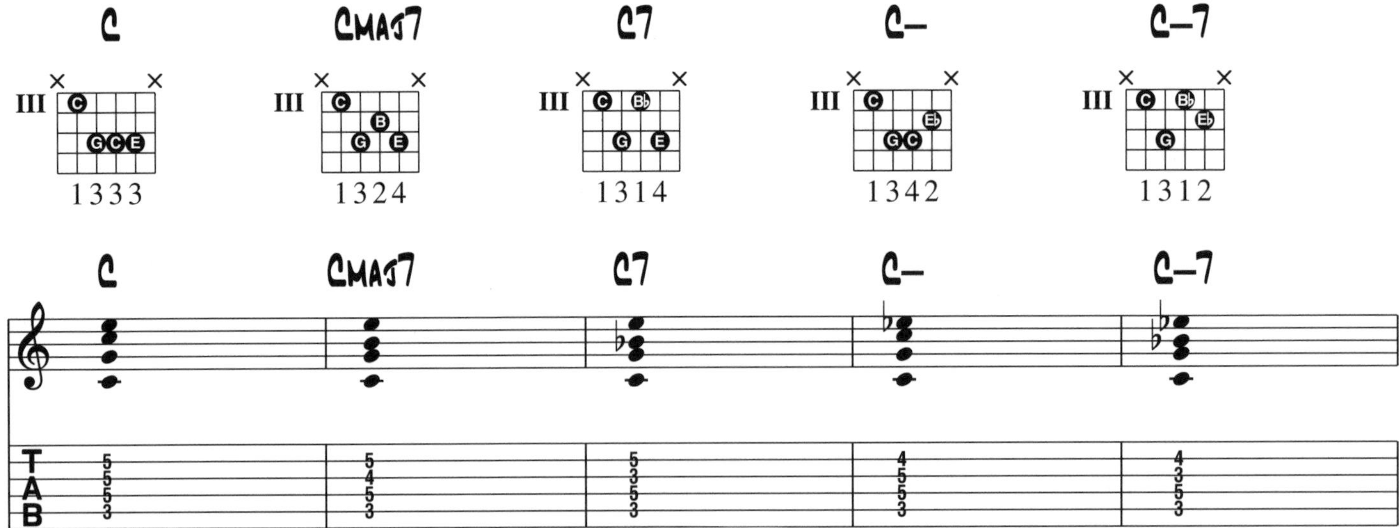

PRACTICE TIP

Developing new fingering techniques like these takes steady practice over a long period of time. Practice these chord forms every day. Over time, they will become easier.

Root on Sixth String

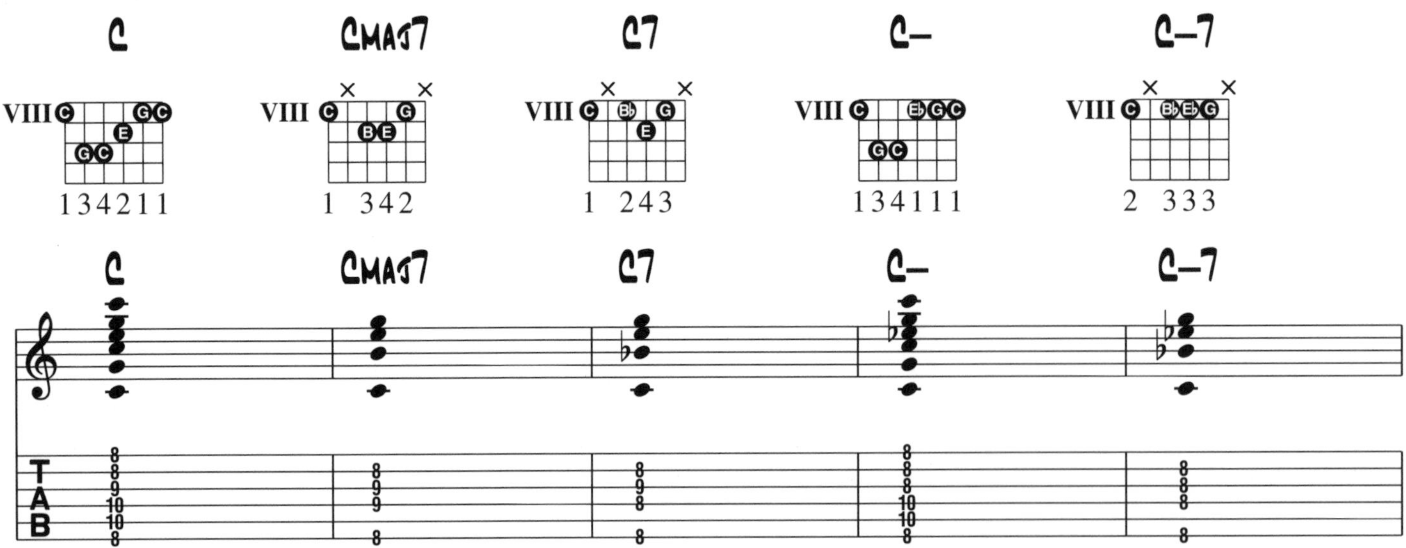

CHORD FORM PRACTICE

Practice this exercise very slowly, at first. First, use chord forms with the root on the fifth string. Then use chord forms with the root on the sixth string. Start this next exercise with simple rhythms—steady whole notes or half notes. As you begin to feel more comfortable playing the different chord forms, you can make the rhythms more complex. Play rhythms from your comping part, or any rhythms of your choice. Whichever rhythms you choose, play the same rhythm in every measure.

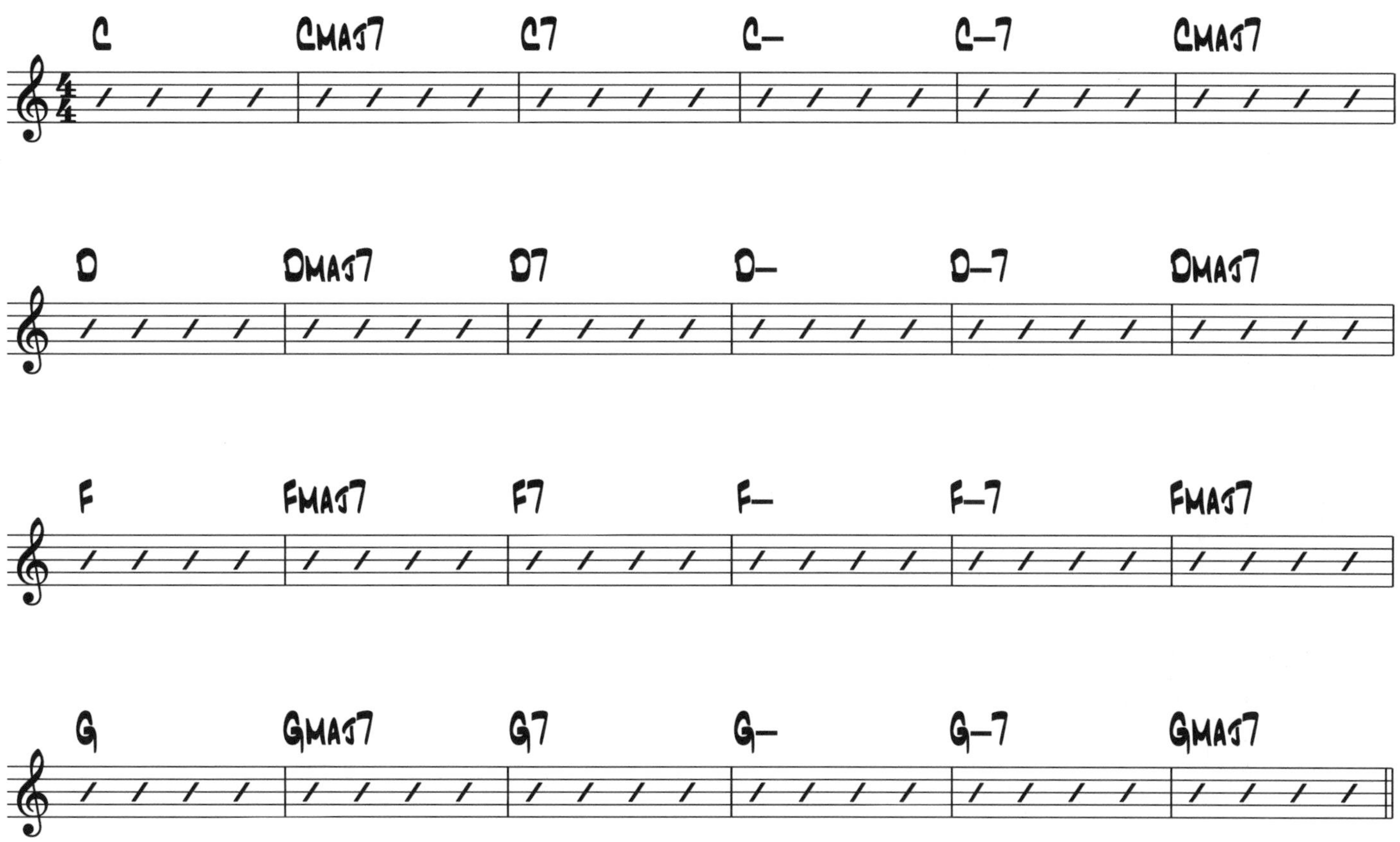

MOVABLE SCALES

In the same way that fingerings for some chords can be movable, the fingerings for some scales are also movable. In lesson 27, you learned the D major pentatonic scale. The same fingering, 1–3–1–4–1–4, can begin on any fret. As long as you begin on the third string, this fingering will always play a major pentatonic scale. Practice major pentatonic scales beginning on every fret.

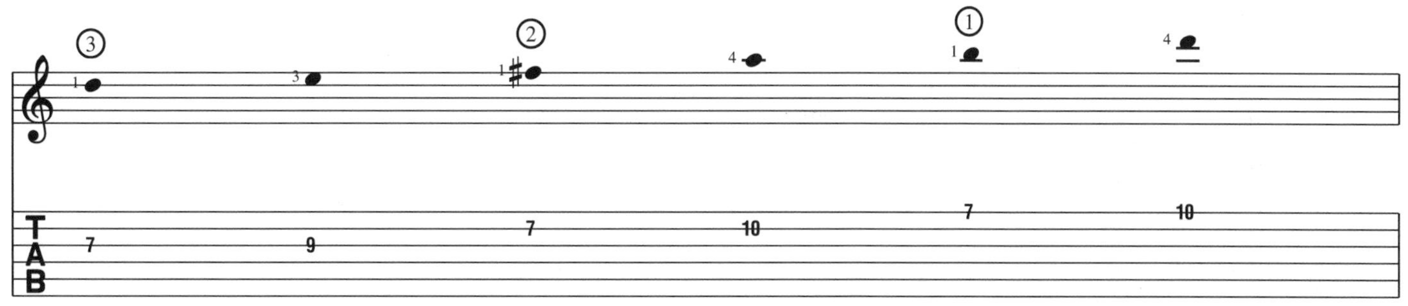

PENTATONIC PRACTICE

Practice each scale slowly, up and down, using the movable scale form shown. Listen to the sound and memorize the fingering. After you have practiced them on the second and fifth frets, try moving each string/finger pattern to other frets.

Second Position | **Fifth Position**

1. Finger Pattern 4-1-3-1-3-2

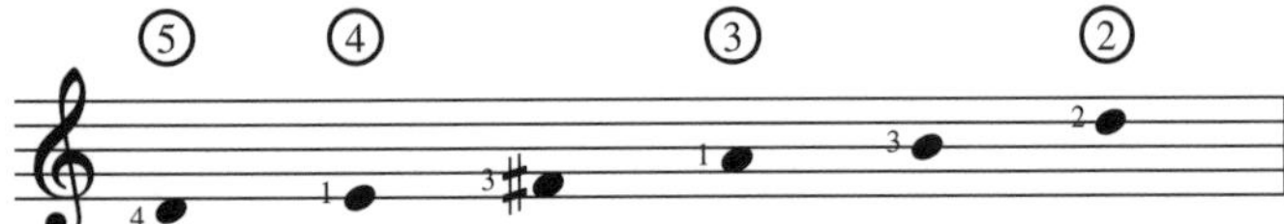

2. Finger Pattern 2-4-1-4-1-4

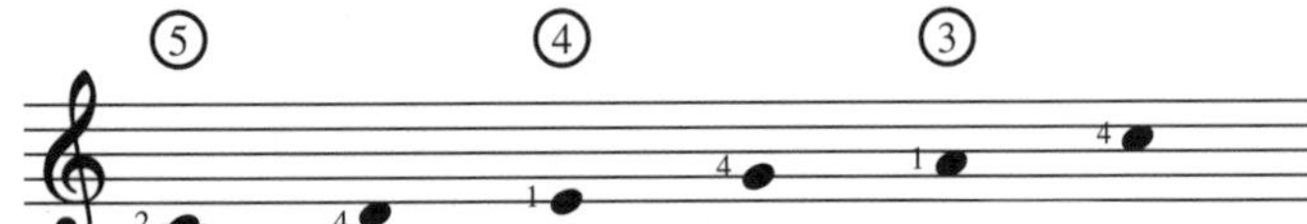

3. Finger Pattern 2-4-1-4-2-1

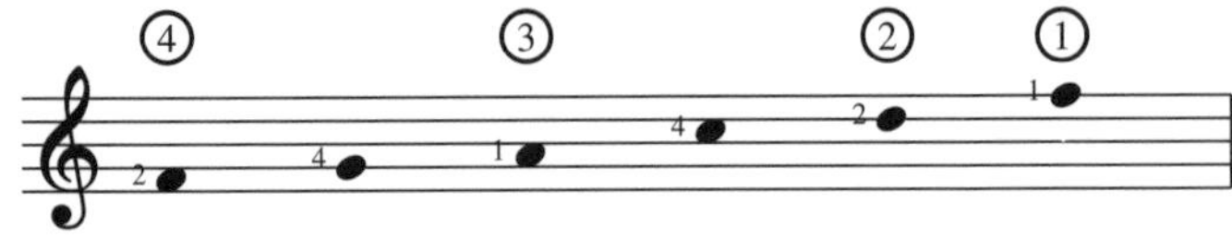

4. Finger Pattern 4-1-3-2-4-2

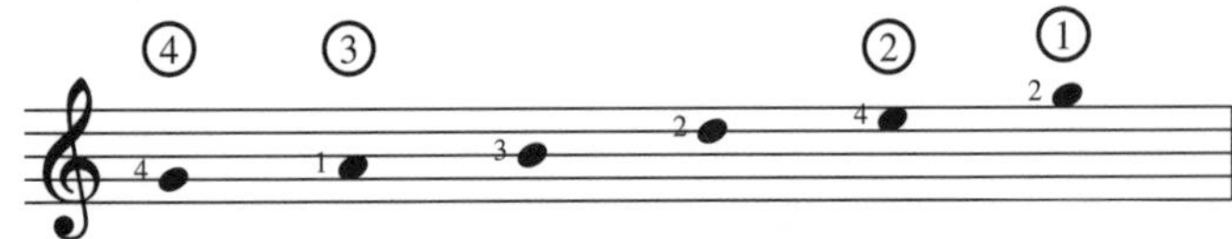

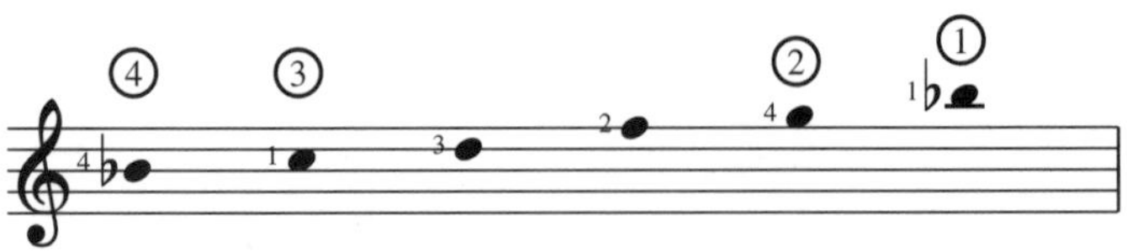

5. Finger Pattern 1-3-1-4-1-4

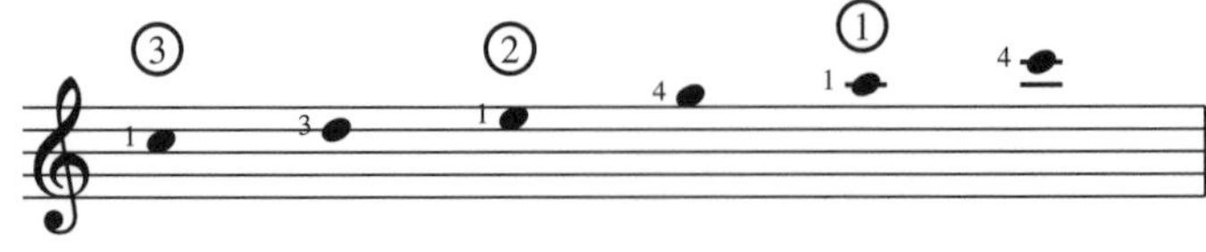

HOOKING UP

A good way to practice hooking up is by imitating the other instruments. Listen to the recording several times. Listen to each member of the rhythm section. Match the rhythms of each instrument's part (playing on muted strings)—first guitar, then bass, then keyboards. Play the track over and over, hooking up with different instruments each time. The better you know the other instruments' parts, the better you can hook up with them.

These are the rhythms of their basic parts:

LISTEN 36 PLAY

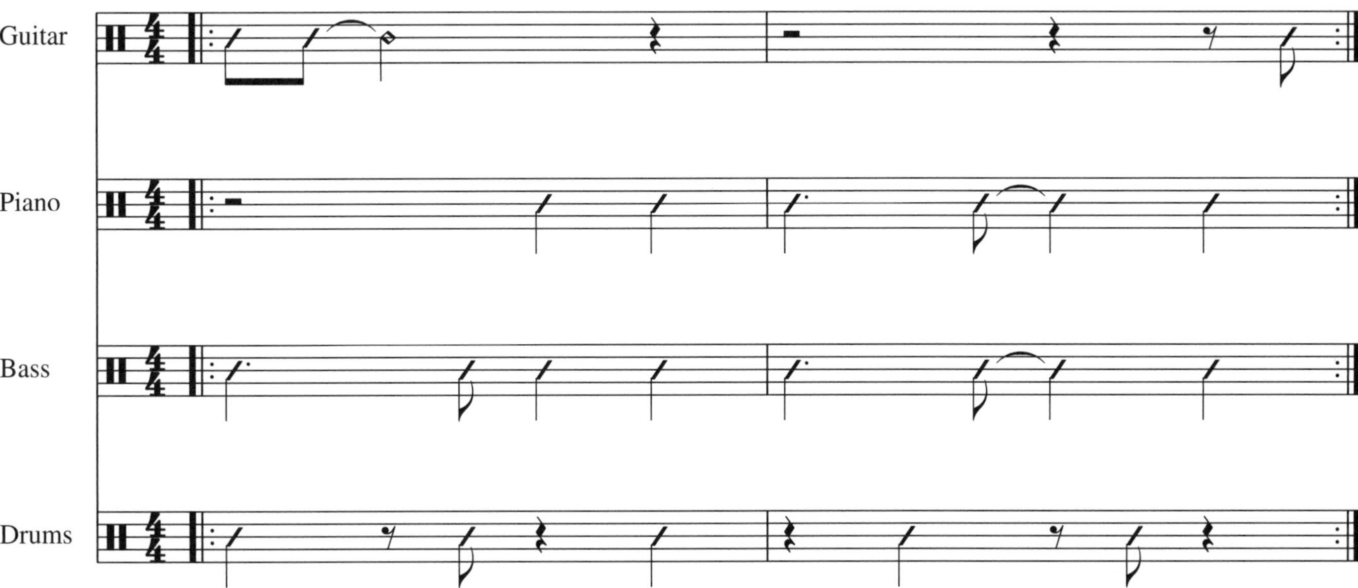

CHALLENGE

Hook up with the drum part in the same way. You may even match the drums one at a time—bass drum, snare (rim click), hi-hat, ride cymbal.

ADDED CHALLENGE

What pitches are the bass and keyboard playing? Try to find the bass notes and the top notes played by the keyboard, and play their parts along with the recording.

MEMORIZE

LISTEN 39 PLAY

Create your own comping part and improvised solo to "Take Your Time." Practice it along with the recording, and memorize it.

Summary

Form
16-Bar AB
(1 chorus = 16 bars)
A: 8 M.
B: 8 M.
Arrangement
Intro: 8 M.
2 Chorus Melody
2 Chorus Solo
1 Chorus Melody
End: 8 M.
Harmony
A
B
D–7 E♭maj7 Dmaj7
Scale
D Minor Pentatonic
D Major Pentatonic

Play "Take Your Time" with your own band!

PLAYING STOP TIME

"Stop It" is a blues/jazz tune in which *stop time* accents the melody, like a question and answer. Stop time is very common in blues, jazz, and other styles. To hear more stop time blues, listen to artists such as Miles Davis, John Coltrane, Jim Hall, Sarah Vaughn, Bill Evans, Ella Fitzgerald, Louis Armstrong, Abbie Lincoln, Dizzy Gillespie, and Charlie Parker.

LESSON 29
TECHNIQUE/THEORY

Listen to "Stop It" and then play along with the recording. At the head, the guitar plays this melody. Play it in fifth position.

LISTEN 40 PLAY

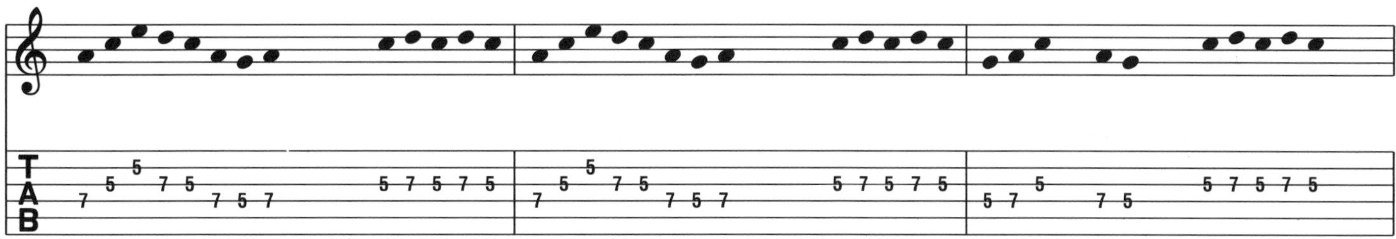

When other instruments are soloing, the guitar comps chords.

A–7 D–7 E7(♯9)

	A–7	D–7	E7(♯9)
T	5	6	8
A	5	5	7
	5	7	6
B	5	5	7

MELODY

Legato

LISTEN 41 PLAY

Listen to the first three notes of "Stop It." The first three notes should be played *legato*—smooth and connected. To play legato:

1. Use separate strings (strings 4, 3, and 2).
2. Use rest strokes, letting the pick fall directly to the next string.
3. Glide the pick across the strings, rather than hitting or plucking them.

The second part of this phrase is made up of five notes. Play it on strings 3 and 4, using alternate picking, and keep your hand in the same position. This fingering will help you play legato, and also will help you play the lick quickly. Practice each string individually. Then practice the entire lick.

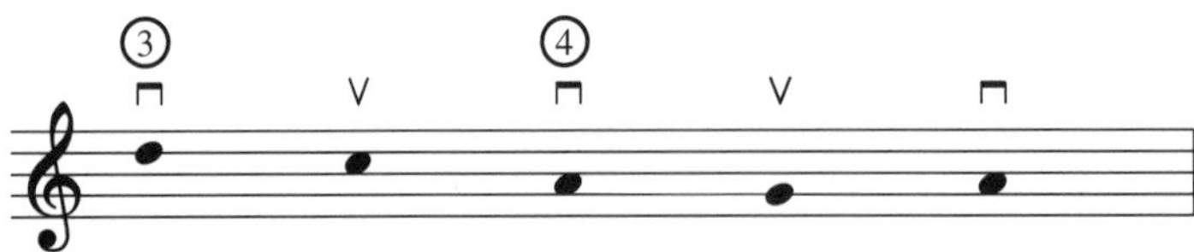

When you can play both licks easily, put them together and play them along with the recording. Hold the last note as long as it is held in the recording. This phrase is played twice.

HAMMER ON

For the third phrase, you will use *hammer-on* technique. When you "hammer on" a string, you sound the note with fingers of your left hand, striking the string sharply against the fingerboard.

Play an open-string G (third string), and then play an A on the same string by hammering on the second fret. Do not pick the second note. Notice how legato the two notes sound. Notes meant to be hammered are often shown with a *slur* (curved line) connecting them.

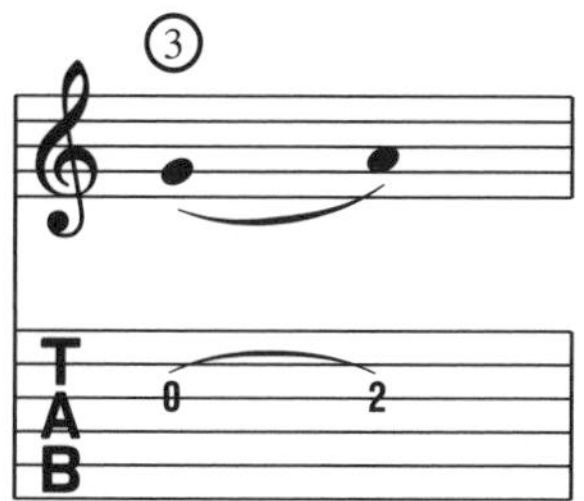

Now, move to the fourth string, fifth fret, and play the same two notes. Pluck the G (fifth fret), but hammer on the A (seventh fret).

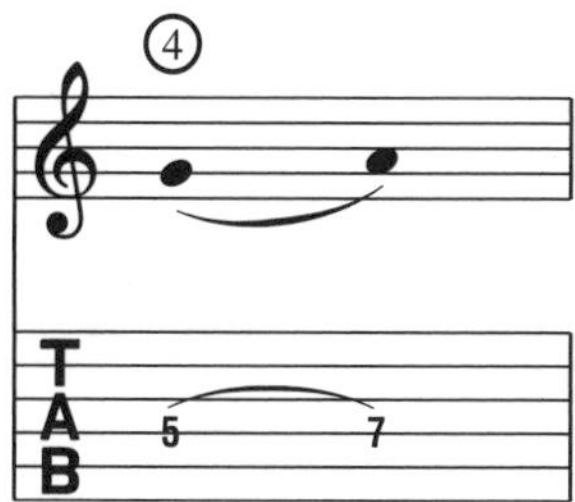

Notice there is no picking indicated for the second note. Instead, hammer on the A. After picking the first note, drop your third finger sharply on the fret of the next note—hard enough to sound the note without picking with the right hand.

PRACTICE TIP

Strive for an even sound on both the plucked note and the hammered note. While you hammer-on with your third finger, hold your first finger on the note you just picked.

Try the melody's third phrase, using the fingering and picking shown below. Hammer on the slurred notes.

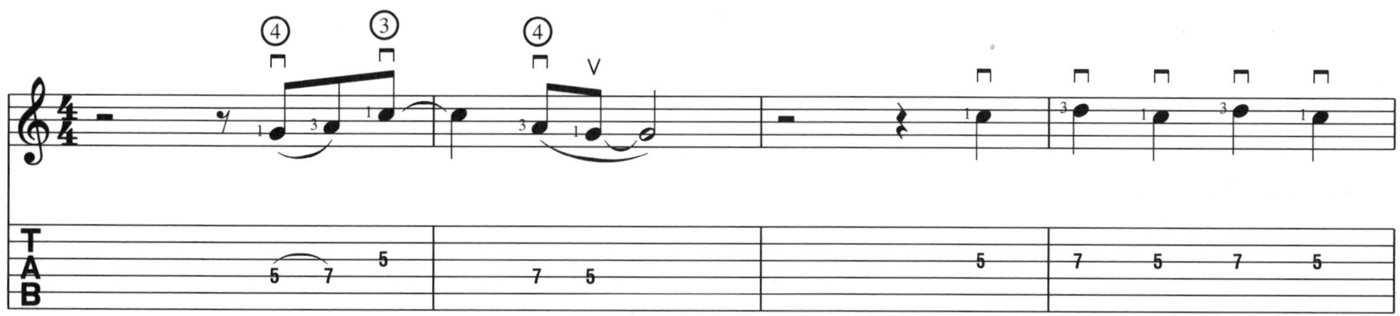

COMPING

The three chords used in "Stop It" are A–7, D–7, and E7(♯9).

LISTEN 42 PLAY

1. Play each chord. Practice switching from one to another.

2. At the end of each stroke, rest your pick on the first string. This emphasizes the chord's top note.

3. Listen to the recording, and notice the top note of the chords played by the guitar and keyboard. Sing along with these notes.

4. Play along with the recording. Match the rhythm of the recorded guitar part. Make sure your chords do not ring longer than those in the recording.

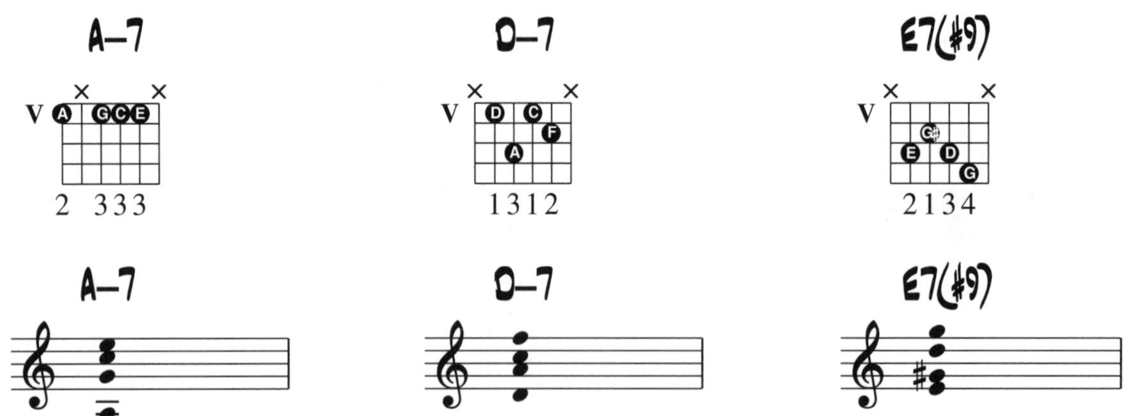

LESSON 30
LEARNING THE GROOVE

HOOKING UP TO STOP-TIME BLUES

LISTEN 40 PLAY

Listen to "Stop It." This jazz cymbal beat is at the heart of jazz rhythm. The "spang spang a-lang" cymbal beat is unique to jazz, and it has been its primary pattern since the 1940s. Its underlying pulse is the same as the shuffle. This pattern has accompanied Louis Armstrong, Count Basie, Miles Davis, John Coltrane, Duke Ellington, and thousands of other jazz artists.

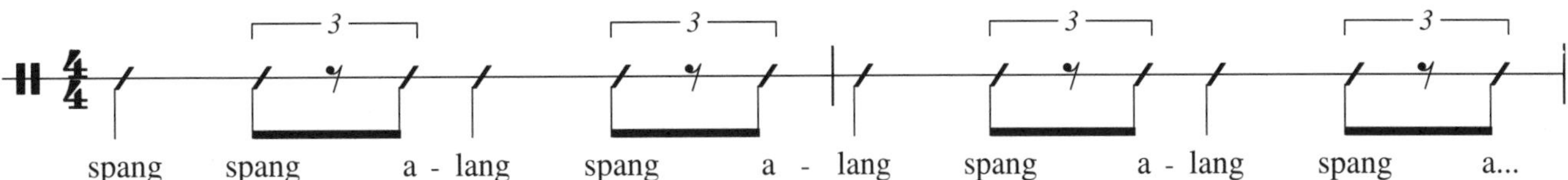

STOP TIME

LISTEN 41 PLAY

In stop time, the groove is punctuated by *stop time kicks*. These are rhythmic figures, usually just one or two beats long, that punctuate the melody. That is why it is called "stop time"—the melody "stops" or rests.

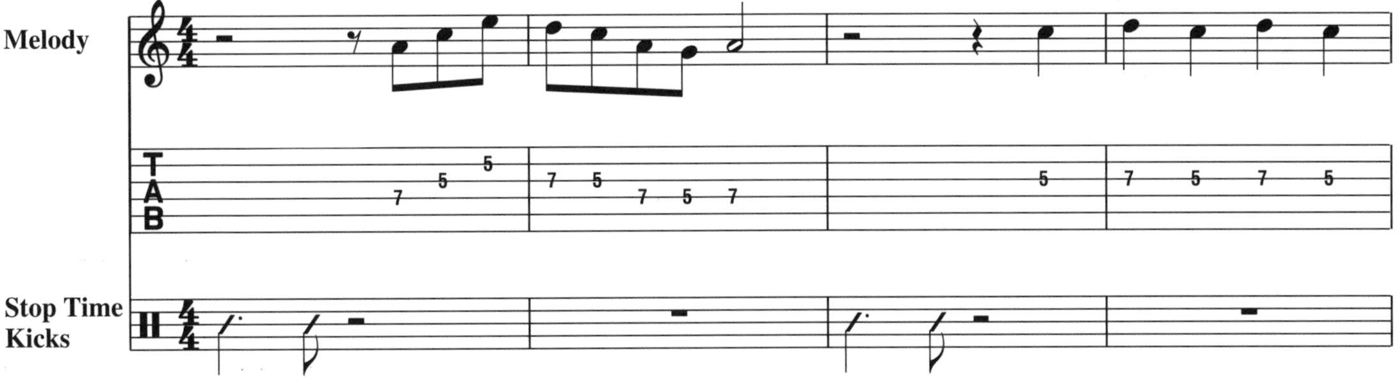

REGULAR TIME

LISTEN 42 PLAY

During the solos, the rhythm section *plays time*. The drums play a steady beat and the bass *walks* (plays steady quarter notes).

LISTEN 43 PLAY

Play along with the recording, and match the guitar part in both sections. On this tune, the guitar plays melody during the stop time sections. During the solos, it plays a comping part. Tap the pulse with your foot, and count the subdivisions. Hook up with the groove, and notice how the guitar and keyboard connect during the solo sections. Compare the rhythms you have been playing with the written part in lesson 32.

LESSON 31
IMPROVISATION

FORM AND ARRANGEMENT

Listen to "Stop It" and try to figure out the form and arrangement by ear. Check your answer against the summary at the end of this chapter.

LISTEN 40 PLAY

IDEAS FOR IMPROVISING

Use the A blues scale to improvise over this tune.

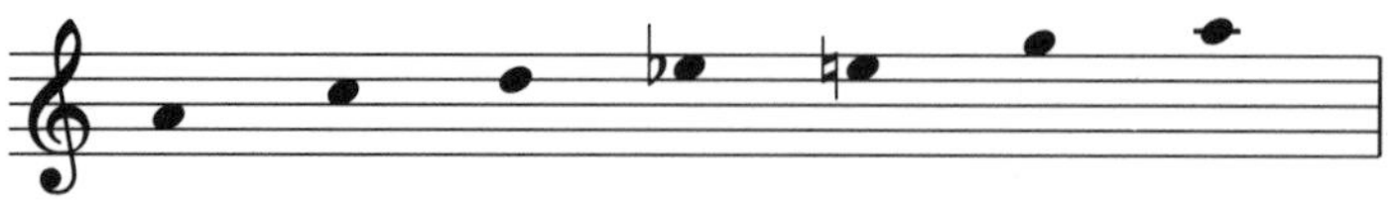

CALL AND RESPONSE

1. Echo each phrase, exactly as you hear it.
2. Improvise an answer to each phrase. Imitate the sound and rhythmic feel of the phrase you hear, and use the notes from the A blues scale.

LISTEN 44 PLAY

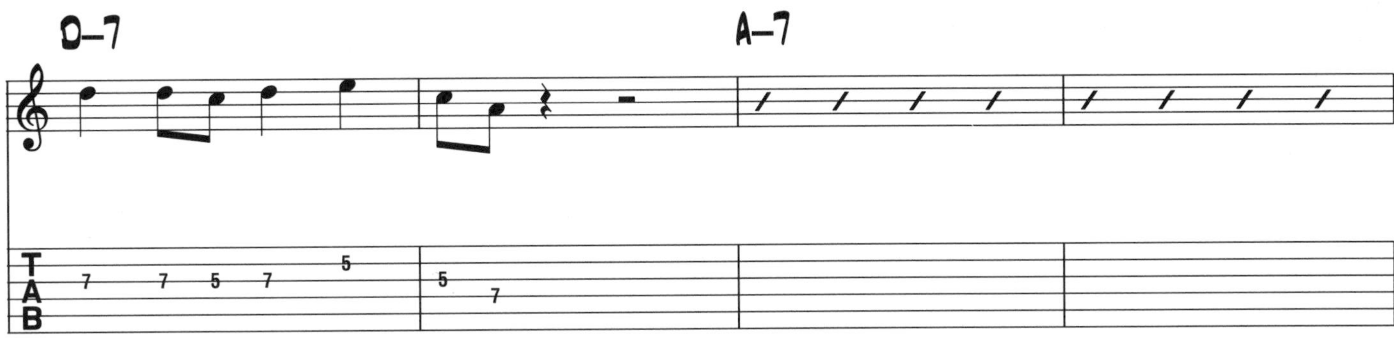

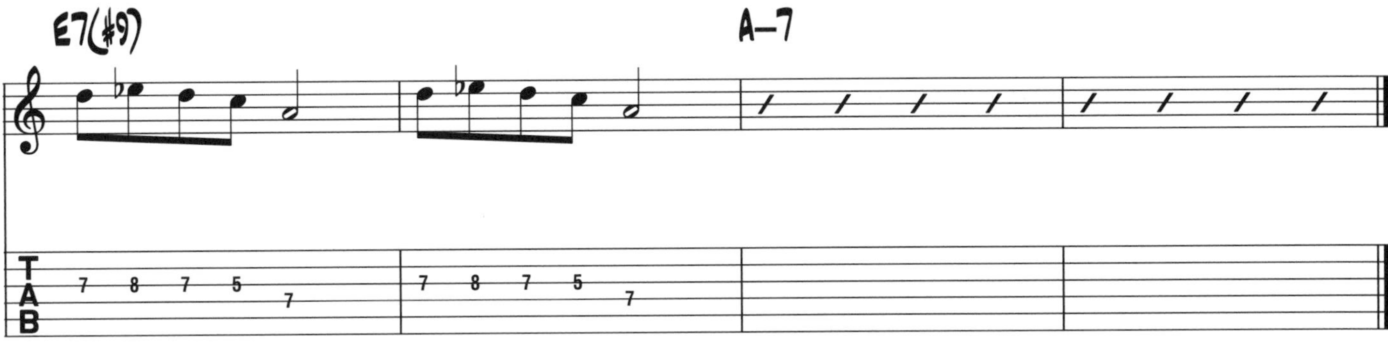

LISTEN 45 PLAY

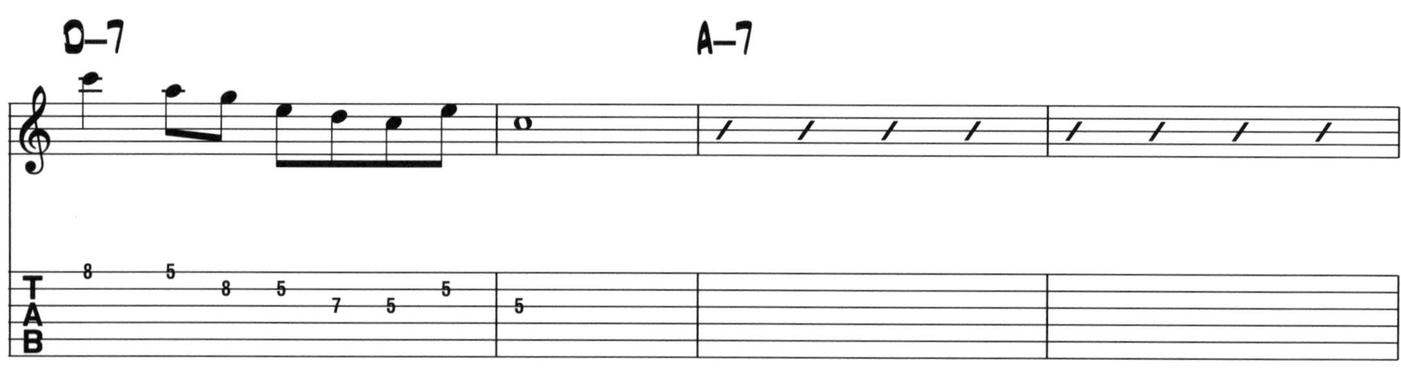

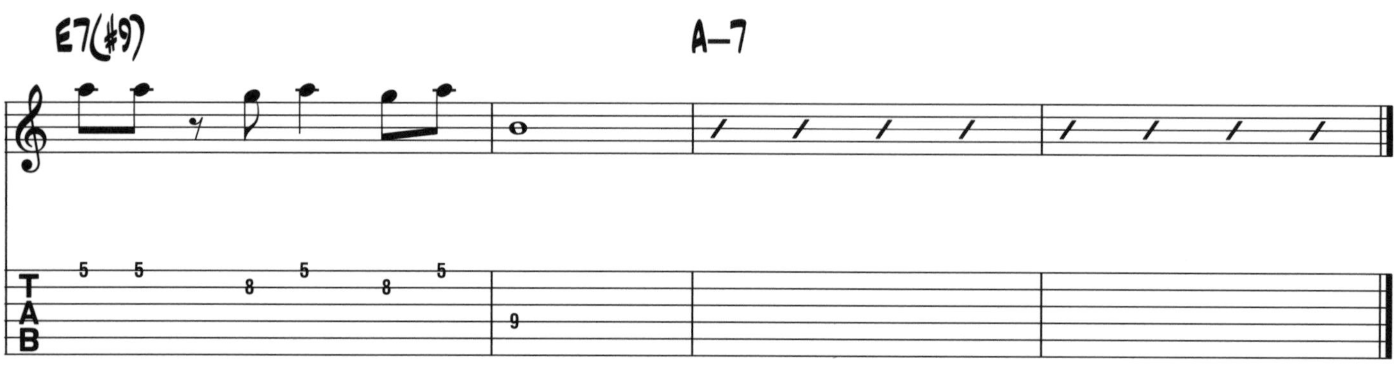

Write out a few of your own ideas. Use the A blues scale.

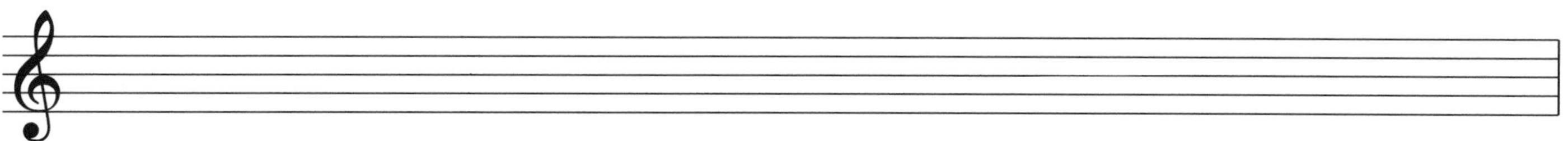

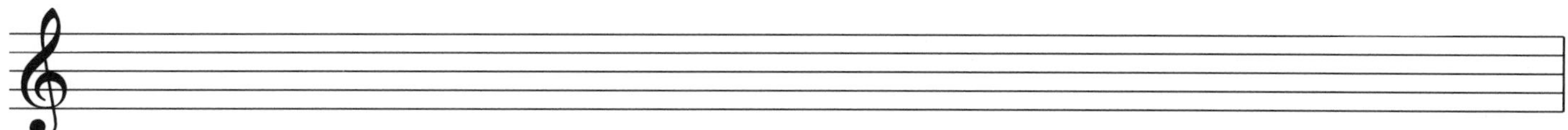

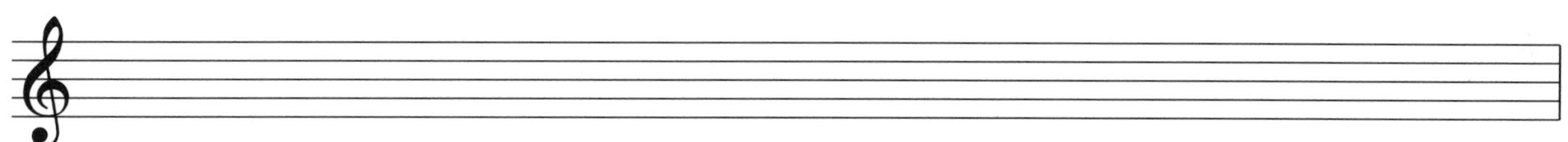

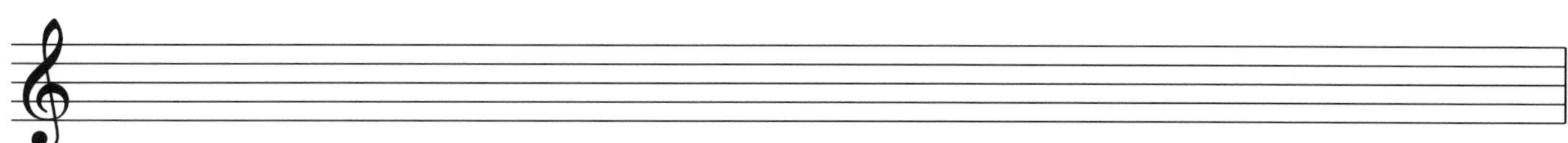

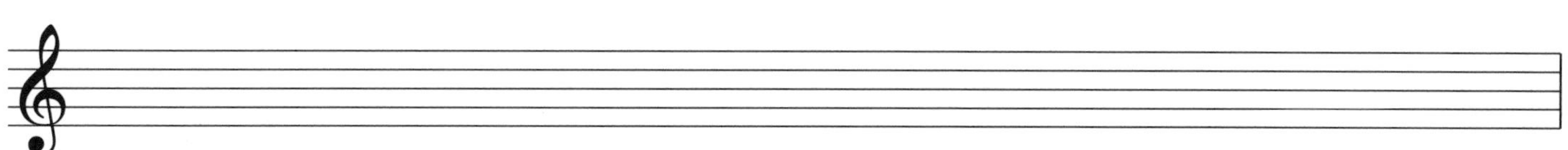

LISTEN 43 PLAY

Create a one-chorus solo using any techniques you have learned. Memorize your solo and practice it along with the recording.

LESSON 32
READING

GUITAR PART

D.C. AL ⊕ From the beginning, and take the coda. Jump to the very first measure of the tune and play from there. When you reach the first coda symbol, skip ahead to the next coda symbol (at the end). This is similar to the "D.S. al Coda," but instead of going to a sign, go to the first measure of the tune.

Play "Stop It" along with the recording and read from the written guitar part.

Stop It

Guitar Part

By Matt Marvuglio

"Swing" ♩ = 156

A

A–7

Melody

Guitar

D–7

A–7

E7(#9)

A–7

To Coda ⊕

B
SOLOS
A–7
D–7
A–7
E7(#9)
A–7
AFTER SOLOS, D.C. AL
CODA

LEAD SHEET

Play "Stop It" from the lead sheet. Use your own comping part. Notice that the lead sheet is written an octave lower than your guitar part. Feel free to change the octave to make it suit the guitar better.

LISTEN 43 PLAY

By Matt Marvuglio

"Swing" ♩ = 156

DAILY PRACTICE ROUTINE

CHORD PRACTICE

The next exercise will help you practice switching between chords. You will play A–7, B–7 (♭5), CMA7, D–7, and E7(♯9). These are movable chord forms, which you can play in any position.

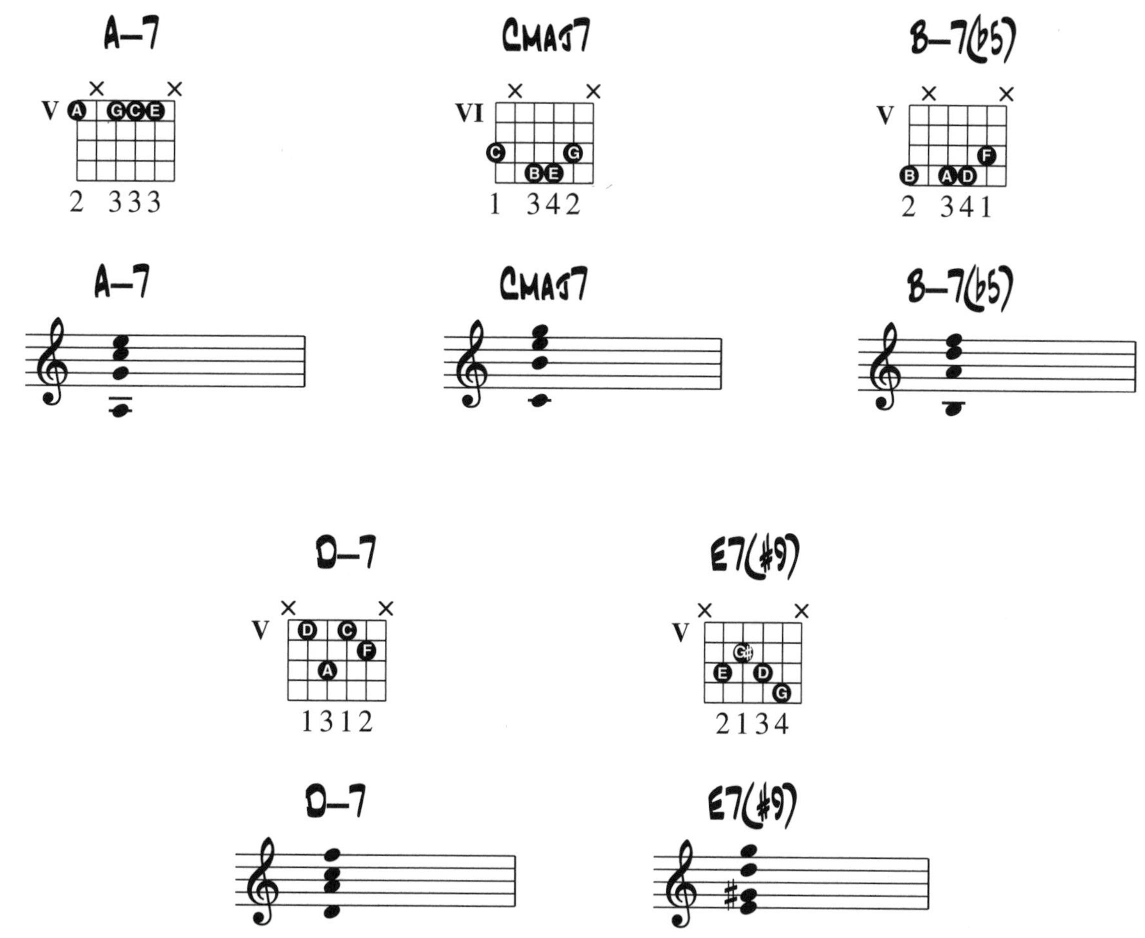

PRACTICE TIP

When changing chords, imagine the new chord form before playing it. Finger the new chord mid-air, before actually touching the strings.

CHORD PRACTICE

Practice changing chords until you can play them easily.

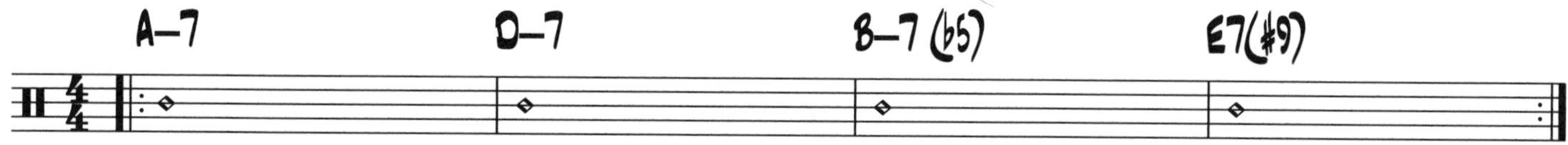

Blues

Practice these chords in a blues progression. Use a metronome, and play slowly at first, keeping a steady beat. If you miss a beat, start again, but more slowly. When you can play it perfectly, increase the tempo. After you play it with the metronome, play it along with the recording.

LISTEN 43 PLAY

Whole Notes

Half Notes

Quarter Notes

Accent the backbeat.

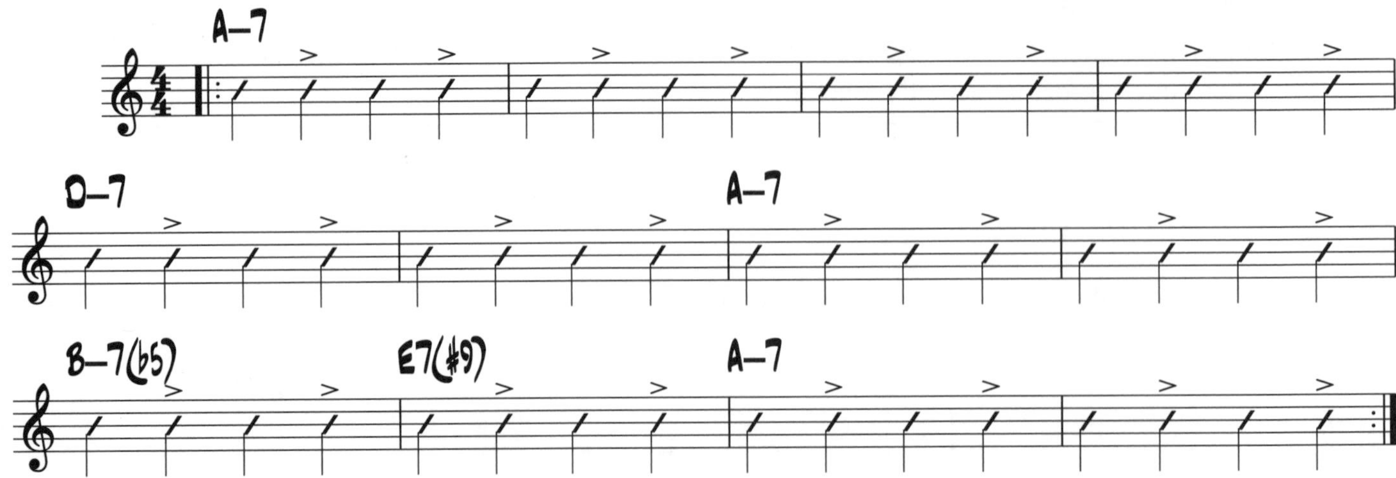

Your Own Rhythm

Use your own comping rhythms.

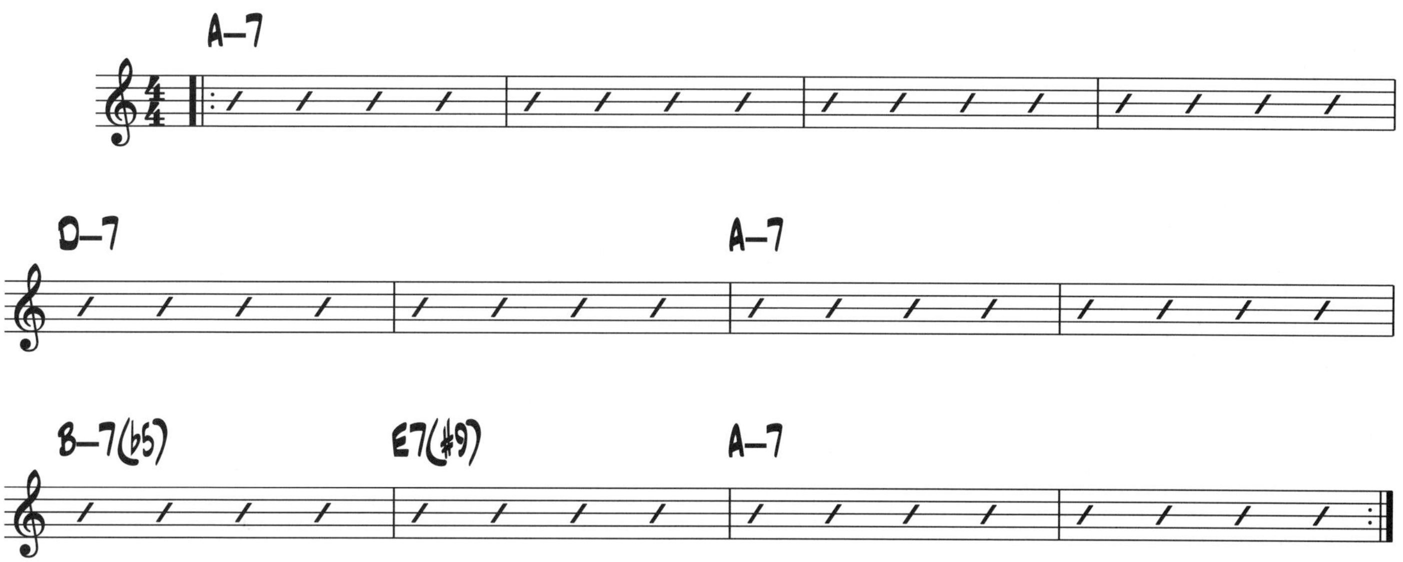

SWING PRACTICE

This exercise will help you keep a steady tempo and develop a swing feel. In swing, the drummer often empahsizes beats 2 and 4. With the metronome beating quarter notes, strum chords on every beat, and accent beats 2 and 4.

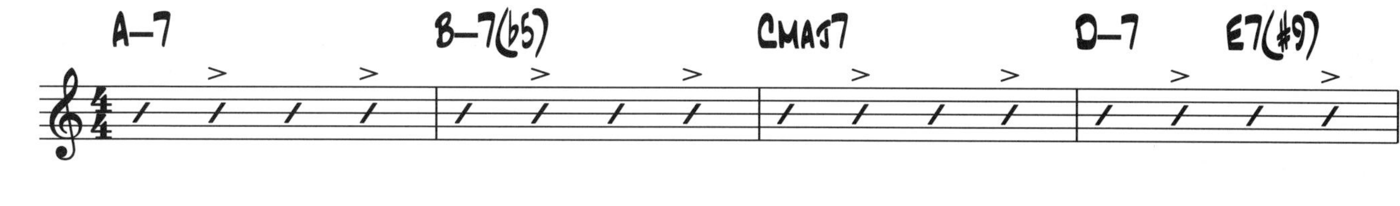

CALL AND RESPONSE

1. Echo each phrase, exactly as you hear it.
2. Improvise an answer to each phrase. Imitate the sound and rhythmic feel of the phrase you hear, and use the notes from the A blues scale.

Write out a few of your own ideas. Use the A blues scale.

LISTEN 43 PLAY

Create a one-chorus solo using any techniques you have learned. Memorize your solo and practice it along with the recording.

SOLO PRACTICE

Practice this melody and play it along with the recording. It is based on the A blues scale.

LISTEN 43 PLAY

MEMORIZE

LISTEN 43 PLAY

Create your own comping part and improvised solo to "Stop It." Practice it along with the recording, and memorize it.

SUMMARY

FORM
12-BAR BLUES
(1 CHORUS = 12 BARS)

ARRANGEMENT
2 CHORUS MELODY
4 CHORUS SOLO
2 CHORUS MELODY
END: 1 M.

HARMONY

SCALE

PLAY "STOP IT" WITH YOUR OWN BAND!

FINAL REMARKS

Congratulations on completing the *Berklee Practice Method.* You now have a good idea of the role of the guitarist in a band, and have command of the eight grooves/time feels of these tunes. The melodies and the harmonic progressions that you have learned are important and useful parts of your musical vocabulary. In addition, you have tools and ideas for creating your own comping parts and solos. This is a great start!

What to do next? Play along with your favorite recordings. Find records that you hear other musicians talking about. Learn these tunes, grooves, and comping parts. There is a good reason that musicians talk about certain bands, albums, or guitarists. Continue your theory, reading, and technique work. Investigate chord scales and modes. Learn all your key signatures (major and minor), scales, and chord arpeggios.

Develop your concept of what it means to play guitar. Realize how important you are as a guitarist in a band. You have a big responsibility, taking care of the melody, the harmony, and the groove. It is a powerful position.

Play your guitar every day, by yourself and with others, and get the sound in your body.

Keep the beat!

—Larry